How Great Leaders Think

Peter
you are great
and your work
in expanding the
leadership distar
of physicians
magic

How Great Leaders Think

The Art of Reframing

Lee G. Bolman • Terrence E. Deal

JB JOSSEY-BASS™
A Wiley Brand

Cover design by Wiley
Cover image © Tetra Images/Getty Images

Published by Jossey-Bass
A Wiley Brand
One Montgomery Street, Suite 1200, San Francisco, CA 94104-4594—www.josseybass.com

Jossey-Bass books and products are available through most bookstores. To contact Jossey-Bass directly call our Customer Care Department within the U.S. at 800-956-7739, outside the U.S. at 317-572-3986, or fax 317-572-4002.

Wiley publishes in a variety of print and electronic formats and by print-on-demand. Some material included with standard print versions of this book may not be included in e-books or in print-on-demand. If this book refers to media such as a CD or DVD that is not included in the version you purchased, you may download this material at http://booksupport.wiley.com. For more information about Wiley products, visit www.wiley.com.

Library of Congress Cataloging-in-Publication Data
Bolman, Lee G.
    How great leaders think : the art of reframing / Lee G. Bolman, Terrence E. Deal.
      pages   cm
    Includes index.
    ISBN 978-1-118-14098-7 (hardback); ISBN 978-1-118-28450-6; ISBN 978-1-118-28223-6
  1. Leadership.   2. Organizational change.   I. Deal, Terrence E.   II. Title.
HD57.7.B6393 2014
658.4'092–dc23

                                                      2014013595

Printed in the United States of America

FIRST EDITION
HB Printing   10 9 8 7 6 5 4 3 2 1

CONTENTS

PREFACE

This book has a simple message:

- Good thinking is the starting point for good leadership.

- Leaders who can reframe—look at the same thing from multiple perspectives—think better. They create a lucid portrait of what's going on around them and have a clearer vision of what's needed to achieve desired results.

- Leaders can see and do more when they know how to negotiate four key areas of the leadership terrain: structural, human resource, political, and symbolic.

This book answers a request we've often heard from readers and fans of our work who have asked for a shorter, more applied version of *Reframing Organizations*. This new book is a compact overview of our ideas about reframing and our four-frame model, with a focus on leadership. Because storytelling is often the best form of teaching, we use cases and examples, many of them from iconic leaders, to provide realistic lessons about how great leaders think and act.

This work appears thirty years after we published our first book (with the ungainly title *Modern Approaches to Understanding and Managing Organizations*). Back then, we hoped we might be onto something. Our ideas were still evolving, but we believed that they captured much of the existing research on organizations and leadership, and we were encouraged by former students who were starting to send positive reports back from the field. We've learned a lot in the years since, and we're even more confident that our framework has breadth and power. Readers, colleagues, students, and workshop participants continue to report that our ideas are useful, even career saving, in the heat of practice. Their support and input has taught us and sustained us along the way. So has our long-term partnership. Book writing can be rewarding, but it's hard work that intersperses epiphanies and moments of joy with roadblocks and dark times when nothing seems to work. It's a lot easier with a partner, and our respect and affection for each other has helped us sustain a mostly long-distance writing relationship through the decades.

ACKNOWLEDGMENTS

We'd like to thank all the people around the world who've contributed to our work, but the list is too long and our memories too short. We've had wonderful colleagues and students at Berkeley, Carnegie-Mellon, Harvard, Stanford, University of La Verne, the University of Missouri–Kansas City, the University of Southern California, Vanderbilt, and Yale, and we're still grateful to all of them. They've given us invaluable criticism, challenge, and support over the years.

Ellen Harris took time away from her work at Harvard and Outward Bound to support this project, offer insights and ideas, and generously give us feedback on our manuscript. As always, Lee is grateful to Dave Brown, Phil Mirvis, Barry Oshry, Tim Hall, Bill Kahn, and Todd Jick of the Brookline Circle, now in its fourth decade of searching for joy and meaning in lives devoted to the study of leadership and organizations.

Many of Lee's colleagues at UMKC's Bloch School have provided invaluable support and input, including Dave Cornell, Nancy Day, Dave Donnelly, Doranne Hudson, Clancy Martin, Dave Renz, Will Self, Marilyn Taylor, and Sidne Ward. Bruce Kay continues to help Lee stay sane and productive.

Lee offers special thanks to Henry Bloch for his friendship and for endowing the Marion Bloch/Missouri Chair that Lee has been honored to occupy since 1993. Henry created the chair in honor of his wife, Marion, a truly remarkable woman who died too soon in 2013.

Terry continues to receive excellent counsel and advice from colleagues scattered in various places: Devorah Lieberman, Jack Meek, Peggy Redman, Donna Redman, and Julie Wheeler, University of La Verne; Sharon Conley, University of California, Santa Barbara; Kent Petersen, emeritus, University of Wisconsin; Warren Bennis, Gib Hentscke, and Stu Gothald, University of Southern California; Regina Pacheco, University of Phoenix; Patrick Faverty and Eric Prather, SLO's Friday Afternoon Think Puddle.

Our lives become more ritualized as we age, and we once again wrapped up a manuscript at the Ritz-Carlton in Phoenix. As always, the staff there made us feel more than welcome and exemplified the Ritz-Carlton tradition of superlative service. Thanks to John Beeson, Grant Dipman, Jean Hengst, Sharon Krull, Rosa Melgoza, Marta Ortiz, Jean Wright, and their colleagues.

The couples of the Edna Ranch Vintners Guild—the Pecatores, Hayneses, Andersons, and Donners—link efforts with Terry in exploring the ups, downs, and mysteries of the art and science of winemaking. Two professional winemakers, Romeo "Meo" Zuech of Piedra Creek Winery and Brett Escalera of Consilience and TresAnelli, offer advice that applies to leadership as well as winemaking. Meo reminds us, "Never overmanage your grapes," and Brett prefaces his answer to every question with "It all depends."

We're delighted to be well into the fourth decade of our partnership with Jossey-Bass. We're grateful to the many friends who have helped us over the years, including Bill Henry, Steve Piersanti, Lynn Luckow, Bill Hicks, Debra Hunter, Cedric Crocker, Byron Schneider, David Brightman, and many others. In recent years, Kathe Sweeney has been a wonderful editor and even better friend, and we're delighted to be working with her again. Rob Brandt, Kathleen Dolan Davies, Mary Garrett, Michele Jones, Nina Kreiden, and Alina Poniewaz have done vital and much-appreciated work backstage in helping get all the pieces together and keep the process moving forward.

We received many valuable suggestions from a diverse, knowledgeable, and talented team of outside reviewers. We did not succeed in implementing all of their many excellent ideas, and they did not always agree among themselves, but the manuscript benefited in many ways from their input.

Lee's six children—Edward, Shelley, Lori, Scott, Christopher, and Bradley—and three grandchildren (James, Jazmyne, and Foster) all continue to enrich his life and contribute to his growth. Terry's daughter, Janie, a chef and TV personality, has a rare talent of almost magically transforming simple ingredients into fine cuisine. Special mention also goes to Terry's parents, Bob and Dorothy Deal. Both are now deceased, but they lived long enough to be pleasantly surprised that their oft-wayward son could write a book. Terry's sister, Patsy, and brother, John, have stood by him in past years when it wasn't clear which direction his life would take.

We say a special thank-you to Chris Argyris, a wonderful and influential colleague and teacher for both of us, who died late in 2013. Chris's mix of playfulness, intellect, and willingness to confront anyone about anything were unique. He's irreplaceable, and we'll miss him.

We again dedicate the book to our wives, who have more than earned all the credit and appreciation that we can give them. Joan Gallos, Lee's spouse and closest colleague, combines intellectual challenge and critique with support and love. Her contributions (which included a very helpful nudge on the question of the book title) have become so integrated into our own thinking that we are no longer able to thank her for all the ways that we have gained from her wisdom and insights.

Sandy Deal's psychological training enables her to approach the field of organizations with a distinctive and illuminating slant. Her successful practice produces examples that have helped us make some even stronger connections to the concepts of clinical psychology. She is one of the most gifted diagnosticians in the field, as well as a delightful partner whose love and support over the long run have made all the difference. She is a rare combination of courage and caring, intimacy and independence, responsibility and playfulness.

To Joan and Sandy, thanks again. As the years accumulate, we love you even more.

PART 1

Leadership in Four Dimensions

Before we change the world, we need to change the way we think.
—Russell Brand[1]

A man cannot expect to progress without thinking.
—Henry Ford[2]

Introduction
The Power of Reframing

Intelligence, talent, and experience are all vital qualities for leadership, but they're not enough. They don't make the difference between success and failure. It's commonplace for businesses, once successful, to go into a funk. Then they need a turnaround because the smart, experienced people in charge who know the place better than anyone else have failed. The usual solution is to bring in an outsider with a stellar track record, but that approach doesn't always work. It all depends on how a leader thinks.

Take the case of an American institution, JCPenney, where generations of Americans had shopped for almost everything for more than a century. More than a few remember it as "the place your mom dragged you to buy clothes you hated in 1984."[1] By 2011, the firm was treading water, and CEO Myron Ullman retired after seven years at the helm. Ullman's initial years had gone well, but the recession of 2008 hit Penney's middle-income shoppers hard, and the company had been going downhill since.

The board looked for a savior and found Ron Johnson, a wunderkind merchant who had worked his magic at two of the most successful retailers in America. He'd made Target hip and led Apple Stores as they became the most profitable retail outlets on the planet. Johnson moved quickly to create a new, trendier JCPenney. His vision went well beyond making the company more profitable. He wanted to graft an entirely new model of retail merchandising on old root stock: "to analysts and employees, Johnson was Willy Wonka asking [them] to go with him on a trip through his retail imagination."[2]

Wanting to move fast, Johnson skipped market tests and staged rollouts. "No need," said Johnson. "We didn't test at Apple."[3] Creative new floor plans divided the stores into boutique shops featuring brands such as Martha Stewart, Izod, Joe Fresh, and Dockers. Centralized locations provided places for customers to lounge, share a cup of coffee, have their hair done, or grab a quick lunch. Games and other entertainment kept children occupied while customers visited boutique offerings or just "hung out."

Johnson quickly did away with Penney's traditional coupons, clearance racks, and sales events, part of a model that relied on inflating prices, then marking them down to create the illusion of bargains. Johnson replaced all that with everyday "Fair and Square" prices. To Johnson's rational way of thinking, this move made perfect sense. But shopping is more of a ritual than a rational undertaking:

> JCP's Ron Johnson was . . . clueless about what makes shopping fun for women. It's the thrill of the hunt, not the buying . . . Women love to shop and deals are what make the game worth playing . . . Bargain hunting is now like playing a game—and finding deeply discounted goods on sale is part of the game.[4]

Johnson replaced much of Penney's leadership with executives from other top retailers. Many, like Johnson, lived in California, far from company headquarters in Plano, Texas. They often looked down on the customers and the JCPenney culture they had inherited. One of Johnson's recruits, COO Michael Kramer, another Apple alum, told the *Wall Street Journal*, "I hated the JC Penney culture. It was pathetic."[5] Inside and outside the company, perceptions grew that Johnson and his crew blamed customers rather than themselves as results went from bad to worse. Traditionally, great merchants, such as Costco's Jim Sinegal or Wal-Mart's Sam Walton, have loved spending time in their stores, chatting up staff and customers, asking questions, and studying everything to stay in touch with their business. Johnson, on the contrary, gave the impression that he wouldn't shop in one of his own stores and didn't particularly understand the people who did.[6]

Johnson substituted broadcasts for store visits. He sent out company-wide video updates every twenty-five days. Staff gathered in training rooms to hear what the CEO had to say, and struggled to make sense of the gap between Johnson's rosy reports and the chaos they were seeing in the stores. It didn't help that Johnson liked to broadcast from his home in Palo Alto or from the Ritz-Carlton in Dallas, where he stayed during visits to headquarters. Instead of marking milestones in Johnson's turnaround effort, the broadcasts deepened a perception that he was out of touch and self-absorbed. They "came to be emblematic of how Johnson seemed to have little grasp of the way he was perceived inside the company and how little faith workers had in his plans."[7]

Johnson's reign at JCPenney lasted seventeen months. Customers left, sales plummeted, and losses piled up. A board with few good options sacked Johnson and reappointed Ullman, the man who had left under a cloud less than two years earlier.

If Johnson failed, even though he was a retail superstar, imagine how much worse it would be for a company to hire a chief executive who didn't even know the business. That's what the board of IBM did after the company ran up a $5 billion loss in 1992. They fired CEO John Akers and went after such luminaries as Jack Welch and Bill Gates, who all said no. Eventually they turned their sights on Lou Gerstner, who had just finished a stint as CEO of Nabisco, purveyor of brands such as Oreos and Triscuit. Skeptics wondered if he knew the difference between chocolate chips and computer chips.

Gerstner spurned the initial overtures. He knew IBM was in deep trouble and wondered whether he, or anyone else, could save it. In the end he was persuaded by friends who told him, "IBM is a national treasure."[8] He took on the awesome challenge of pulling a giant enterprise out of its free fall.

When he arrived at IBM, Gerstner saw an exclusive club of sovereign fiefdoms, a bloated whale trying to compete with a group of agile blue-fin tuna. The smart money wanted to break up the company, and vultures circled in the hope of grabbing the good stuff, like the renowned T. J. Watson Research Center.

In the 1960s and 1970s, IBM had been the jewel of American business, the world's most admired company. Its laboratories developed products such as the System/360 mainframe, so advanced that competitors struggled to keep up. IBM's sales force dominated the computer market. Impeccable customer service kept customers loyal and satisfied, as reflected in the popular adage that "no one ever got fired for buying IBM." Enjoying a near-monopoly in the computer industry, IBM entertained America with Charlie Chaplin commercials and pithy slogans such as THINK. But too much success can be heady and dangerous. IBM began to lose touch with changes in the world outside. Events soon came knocking.

In 1969, the U.S. government slammed IBM with an antitrust suit that dragged on for thirteen years before ending with a whimper. In the meantime, the suit ate cash, distracted management, and made the company gun-shy about doing anything that might bring the feds back. Once a sure-footed market leader, IBM became a laggard as the pace of technological change accelerated. The introduction of the UNIX operating system, championed by HP and Sun, provided a cost-effective option that eroded IBM's dominance in mainframes. IBM fell behind Digital Equipment Corporation as minicomputers grabbed market share, and stumbled badly when personal computers took off.

Enter Gerstner, trained as an engineer at Dartmouth, with a reputation as a hard-nosed rationalist and brilliant strategist who prized analysis, measurement, and discipline. He was known more for impatience and arrogance than charm:

> No one in his right mind would describe a session with Gerstner as congenial. Before he meets with almost anyone, he requires something in writing that establishes the facts, defines the problems, and allows him to skip the small talk when he sees you . . . "When you got a call from Lou, it was never to hear a compliment," recalls [a former subordinate]. "It was always: 'What the hell is this?'"[9]

Gerstner seemed to confirm this tough, rational frame of mind in one of his early comments after coming on board: "The last thing IBM needs right now is a vision."[10]

Gerstner spent his early days getting to know his new place. He traveled to IBM locations in the United States and abroad. He met with stakeholders inside the company and customers outside. Within his first ninety days, he developed five bullet points that defined an initial strategic direction:[11]

- Keep the company together and not spin off the pieces.
- Reinvest in the mainframe.
- Remain in the core semiconductor technology business.
- Protect fundamental R&D budget.
- Drive all we did from the customer back and turn IBM into a market-driven rather than an internally-focused, process-driven enterprise.

The first four might sound like clinging to the past, but all ran counter to conventional wisdom at the time. The fifth point on customer focus signaled that IBM needed to change its ways. These points were only a start. Gerstner knew he had to do much more to revive the "national treasure."

One issue that soon got his attention was culture. In his early days, Gerstner felt as if he had landed on a strange island where the natives spoke a peculiar language and cherished mysterious customs and rituals. Group presentations relied on "foils" that signaled the presenter's place in the social order. "Non-concur" was IBM-speak for "no," and was widely used to delay or kill new initiatives. Phrases such as "crisp up, tweak, and swizzle," "boil the ocean," and "lobs" made sense only to insiders. On two scheduled visits to IBM facilities, Gerstner found it hard just to get in the building. These experiences nudged him to reframe and to begin to look at IBM through a cultural window:

> I came to see at my time at IBM, that culture is not just one aspect of the game—it is the game. In the end, an organization is nothing more than the collective capacity of its people to create value. Vision, strategy, financial management—any management system, in fact—can set you on the right path and carry you for a while. But no enterprise—whether in business, education, healthcare, or *any* area of human endeavor—will succeed over the long haul if those elements aren't part of its DNA.[12]

Gerstner looked back as well as forward, studying IBM's history to glean the secrets of its prior greatness: "It was a magical time and Thomas Watson Sr.

was the wizard who waved the magic wand creating the enchantment and excitement."[13] In opening a window on the past, he saw that Watson's legacy had lost its original intent and hardened into rigid prescriptions. A core value of excellence had deteriorated into obsessive perfectionism, slowing down the development of new products. (Gerstner once complained that products didn't get launched at IBM; they had to escape.) Respect for the individual had morphed into letting people do whatever they wanted. Superior customer service had come to mean controlling customers and selling them what IBM produced rather than what they needed. Tom Watson had insisted on dark suits and white shirts when that was what the customers wore. By the 1990s, the customers had all gone casual, and "IBMers" stuck out like actors costumed for some other century.

Gerstner came to admire the original meaning of IBM's cultural values and beliefs: "In the end my deepest cultural-change goal was to induce IBMers to believe in themselves again—to believe they had the ability to determine their own fate, and they already knew what they needed to know. It was to shake them out of their depressed stupor and remind them of who they were—you're IBM damn it!"[14]

As his thinking expanded beyond analysis and logic to culture and heart, Gerstner developed a symbolic bond with the company: "Along the way, something happened—something that quite frankly surprised me. I fell in love with IBM."[15] In rounding out his traditional strengths in structure and strategy with a new appreciation for the importance of culture and people, Gerstner developed a fuller appreciation of the challenges IBM faced.

Lou Gerstner learned, evolved, and developed a revised picture that enabled him to engineer one of the most successful turnarounds in America's corporate history. Contrast him with Ron Johnson, who approached JCPenney with a heavy dose of rational thinking that he never got beyond. He saw no need to test the assumption that he could make Penney's another Apple. Instead of learning, he discounted contradictory data and remained clueless about the symbolic impact of his moves. Johnson and Gerstner were both smart, experienced leaders with a track record of success who were hired to execute challenging turnarounds. The key difference: Gerstner learned and reframed his thinking. Johnson didn't.

■ ■ ■

The goal of this book is to give you the tools to think like great leaders, whose ability to reframe sets them free, and avoid getting trapped in cognitive ruts. The better you can read and understand your terrain, the clearer you'll be about what to do—like Lou Gerstner. If you misread your situation, you're likely to follow Ron Johnson down a road to ruin. You'll be clueless and won't know what's going wrong. You'll continue doing more of the same even though it's not working. But you won't be alone. There are more Johnsons than Gerstners trying to lead organizations. Why should this be? We'll explore why *cluelessness* is so common.

Then we'll introduce *reframing*—our prescription for sizing things up and figuring out what's really going on. Reframing requires an ability to think about things in more than one way. Gerstner intuitively found another lens when his usual way of making sense was falling short. Leaders can expand how they think by using different mental models to determine what's going on and what to do in complex situations. The goal of this book is to teach you how to do that.

We introduce four distinct and powerful *leadership frames*. Each captures a vital slice of organizational reality. Artfully combined, they enable leaders to develop a more comprehensive view of the challenges and opportunities in whatever situation they face. Gerstner's mastery of this art made him an exemplar of business leadership. You can develop this capacity to think holistically as well.

THE CURSE OF CLUELESSNESS

Year after year, the best and brightest managers maneuver or meander their way to the apex of enterprises great and small. Then, like Ron Johnson, they do really dumb things. Take Bob Nardelli, who expected to win the three-way competition to succeed management legend Jack Welch as CEO of General Electric. Nardelli was stunned when he learned he'd never run GE, but within a week, he received an excellent consolation prize—the top job at Home Depot. He embodied a big change from the company's free-spirited founders, who had built the wildly successful retailer on the foundation of an uninhibited, entrepreneurial "orange" culture. Managers ran their stores using "tribal knowledge," and customers counted on friendly, knowledgeable staff for helpful advice.

Nardelli revamped Home Depot with Six Sigma (an approach he learned at GE) and a heavy dose of command-and-control, discipline, and metrics. Almost all the top executives and many of the frontline managers were replaced, often by ex-military hires. At first, his approach seemed to work—profits improved, and management experts hailed Nardelli's success. But employee morale and customer service went steadily downhill. Where the founders had successfully promoted "make love to the customers," Nardelli's toe-the-line stance pummeled Home Depot to last place in its industry for consumer satisfaction. A new website, HomeDepotSucks .org, gave customers a place to vent their rage.

As criticism grew, Nardelli tried to keep naysayers at bay. At the company's 2006 annual meeting, he gave critics little time to speak and ignored them when they did: "It was, as even Home Depot executives will concede, a 37-minute fiasco. In a basement hotel ballroom in Delaware, with the board nowhere in sight and huge timers on stage to cut off angry investors, Home Depot held a hasty annual meeting last year that attendees alternately described as 'appalling' and 'arrogant.'"[16] The outcry from shareholders and the business press was scathing. Nardelli countered with financial numbers to show that all was well. He seemed unaware or unconcerned that he had embarrassed his board, enraged his shareholders, turned off his customers, and expanded a reputation for arrogance and a tin ear. Like Ron Johnson, he ignored his organization's traditions and culture, and disrespected its people. Nardelli abruptly left Home Depot at the beginning of 2007, and his successor executed a U-turn to take the company back to its historic foundations.

How do bright people turn out so dim? Are they too smart for their own good? Do personality flaws or their style lead them astray? No—research shows that smart people tend to have fewer hang-ups and to be better at most things than the less gifted. The primary source of cluelessness is not personality, style, or IQ but a failure of "common sense." People are at sea whenever their ways of making sense of the world around them fail. They see and imagine the wrong thing, so they do the wrong thing. But if they don't realize that their image is incorrect, they don't understand why they don't get what they hoped for. So they blame someone else and, like Ron Johnson and Bob Nardelli, insist that they're right even when they're headed over a cliff.

FRAMING

A wise and successful executive got to the heart of the challenge managers face every day: "The world simply can't be made sense of, and facts can't be organized, unless you have a mental model to begin with."[17] In his best-seller *Incognito*, David Eagleman writes that human thinking and perception don't work the way most people assume they do. Common sense, for example, tells you that vision is very simple: you look at something and see it. Not so, says Eagleman. Instead, your brain is always looking for matches between what's out there and what's inside. The brain pays attention to differences between what it expects and what's there. It's an efficient process that can be very powerful when your mental maps are good, but very poor when they're not. Newborns, for example, can't tell the difference between their mother's face and a pumpkin because they haven't yet developed their visual software. Chess masters, in contrast, can instantly recognize more than fifty thousand configurations of a chessboard. That's why grand masters can play twenty-five lesser opponents simultaneously, beating all of them while spending only seconds on each move.[18]

Neuroscientists now tell us that believing is seeing rather than the reverse. The human brain constructs its own images of reality and then projects them onto the external world. Reality is what each of us believes it to be: "Beliefs come first, explanations for beliefs follow."[19] Our mental models—rich or impoverished—determine the breadth and depth of our personal reality. How you think determines what you see and how you respond to situations.

There are many labels for such mental models: maps, paradigms, mindsets, worldviews, and cognitive lenses, to name a few. We call them *frames*. A frame is a set of beliefs and assumptions that you carry in your head to help you understand and negotiate some part of your world. A good frame makes it easier to know what's happening, see more options, and make better choices. Frames are vital because human affairs don't come with computerized navigation systems to guide you turn by turn to your destination. Instead, you need to develop and carry accurate maps in your head.

Such maps make it possible to register and assemble key bits of available data into a coherent pattern—an image of what's going on. When it works fluidly, the process takes the form of "rapid cognition," which Malcolm Gladwell examines in his best seller *Blink*. He describes it as a gift that makes it possible to read "deeply into the narrowest slivers of experience. In basketball, the player who can take in and comprehend all that is happening around him or her is said to have 'court sense.'"[20] In the military, it's called "situational awareness."

The same rapid cognition is at work in the diagnostic categories physicians rely on to evaluate patients' symptoms. The Hippocratic Oath— "Above all else, do no harm"—requires physicians to be confident that they have a good diagnosis before prescribing a remedy. Their skilled judgment draws on a repertoire of categories and clues, honed by training and experience.

But sometimes they get it wrong because their diagnostic categories don't quite work for the situation at hand. They put indicators in the wrong category and lock on to the first answer that seems right, even if a few messy facts don't quite fit. Their mind plays tricks on them, and they ignore any inconvenient data that should tell them they're adrift.

Treating patients is hard enough, but the challenge is even tougher in the workplace because organizations are so complex and the diagnostic categories are less well defined. The quality of your judgments depends on the information at hand, your mental maps, and how well you've learned to use them. Good maps align with the terrain and provide enough detail to keep you on course. If you're trying to find your way around downtown San Francisco, a map of Chicago won't help.

Even with the right map, getting around will be slow and awkward if you have to stop and ponder at every intersection. The ultimate goal is fluid expertise, the sort of know-how that lets you think on the fly and navigate organizations as easily as you drive home on a familiar route. You can make decisions quickly and automatically because you know at a glance where you are and what you need to do next.

There is no shortcut to developing this kind of expertise. It takes effort, time, practice, and feedback. Some of the effort has to go into learning frames and the ideas behind them. Equally important is putting the ideas to use. Experience, one often hears, is the best teacher, but that is true only if you reflect on it and extract its real lessons. It wasn't clear, for example, that Bob Nardelli learned very much from his Home Depot experience. In his next leadership opportunity as CEO of Chrysler, he managed to drive the company into bankruptcy in two years—after he passed on a government loan that would have required a cap on executive pay. His stints at Home Depot and Chrysler combined to earn him spots on at least two lists of the worst American CEOs of all time.[21]

His successor, Sergio Marchionne, took the loan and the pay cap, and brought the company back to profitability. One of the key traits of successful executives is that they never pass up a good learning opportunity.[22]

FRAME BREAKING

Framing involves matching mental maps to situations. Reframing involves shifting frames when circumstances change. But reframing also requires another skill—the ability to break frames. Why do that? A news story from the summer of 2007 illustrates this. Imagine yourself among a group of friends enjoying dinner on the patio of your Washington, D.C., home. An armed, hooded intruder suddenly appears and points a gun at the head of a fourteen-year-old guest. It's a potentially lethal home invasion. "Give me your money," he says, "or I'll start shooting." If you're at that table, what do you do? You could freeze. Or you could try to creatively break frame and put a new spin on the situation. That's exactly what hostess Cristina "Cha Cha" Rowan did.

> "We were just finishing dinner," [she] blurted out. "Why don't you have a glass of wine with us?"
>
> The intruder took a sip of their Chateau Malescot St-Exupéry and said, "Damn, that's good wine."
>
> The girl's father . . . told the intruder . . . to take the whole glass. Rowan offered him the bottle. The would-be robber, his hood now down, took another sip and had a bite of Camembert cheese that was on the table.
>
> Then he tucked the gun into the pocket of his nylon sweatpants.
>
> "I think I may have come to the wrong house," he said, looking around the patio of the home in the 1300 block of Constitution Avenue NE.
>
> "I'm sorry," he told the group. "Can I get a hug?"
>
> Rowan, . . . stood up and wrapped her arms around him. Then [the other guests followed suit].

"That's really good wine," the man said, taking another sip. He had a final request: "Can we have a group hug?"

The five adults surrounded him, arms out.

With that, the man walked out with a crystal wine glass in hand, filled with Chateau Malescot. No one was hurt, and nothing was stolen.

. . . In the alley behind the home, investigators found the intruder's empty crystal wine glass on the ground, unbroken.[23]

After the event, the father of the teenager commented, "There was this degree of disbelief and terror at the same time. Then it miraculously just changed. His whole emotional tone turned—like, we're one big happy family now. I thought: Was it the wine? Was it the cheese?"[24]

The wine and cheese helped, but breaking frame made the key difference. In one stroke, Cha Cha Rowan redefined the situation from "we might all be killed here" to "let's try offering our guest some wine." Like her, artistic managers frame and reframe experience fluidly, sometimes with extraordinary results.

John Lewis, one of Martin Luther King Jr.'s lieutenants, reportedly was with King in a protest march when a Southern redneck confronted him and spit in his face. Lewis was silent for a moment and then asked, "May I borrow your handkerchief?" After a long period of startled staring, the man gave Lewis his handkerchief. A conversation led to a friendship. A final example: A critic once commented to the artist Paul Cézanne, "That doesn't look anything like a sunset." Pondering his painting, Cézanne responded, "Then you don't see sunsets the way I do." Like Cézanne, Lewis, and Rowan, leaders have to find new ways to shift points of view when needed.

Like maps, frames are both windows on a territory and tools for navigation. Each window offers a unique view. Every tool has strengths and limitations. Only experience and practice bring you the adroitness and wisdom to take stock of a situation and use suitable tools with confidence and skill.

FOUR LEADERSHIP FRAMES

Leading in an organization is probably as demanding as anything you have ever tried to do. Not surprisingly, what you read or hear about leadership goes off in many different directions, producing conflicting schools of thought. Each version has its own ideas about how to understand and lead organizations. When you are looking for help, you have to sort through a cacophony of voices and visions.

This book helps you sift through the competing voices and merges them into an inclusive framework embracing four distinctive ideas about leadership. The ideas are powerful enough to capture the subtlety and complexity of leadership, yet simple enough to be helpful. We've combed through oceans of literature so you won't have to. We've distilled our learning from thousands of managers and leaders, and scores of organizations. We've condensed it all into four major frames—structural, human resource, political, and symbolic.[25] Each is used by academics and practitioners alike and found in bound form on the shelves of libraries and bookstores. Books, articles, and training programs typically present one frame or another, isolated from the others. Such single-lens views are exactly what got Johnson and Nardelli in trouble and frustrate other leaders.

To illustrate our point, imagine a harried executive browsing in the management section of her local bookseller on a brisk winter day in 2014. She worries about her company's flagging performance and fears that her job might soon disappear. She spots the black cover of *How to Measure Anything: Finding the Value of "Intangibles" in Business*. Flipping through the pages, she notices chapter titles such as "The Methods of Measurement," "Calibration Exercise," and "The Value of Information for Ranges." She is drawn to such phrases as "A key step in the process is the calculation of the economic value of information. . . [A] proven formula from the field of decision theory allows us to compute a monetary value for a given amount of uncertainty reduction."[26] "This stuff may be good," the executive tells herself, "but it seems a little too stiff and numbers driven."

Next she finds *Lead with LUV: A Different Way to Create Real Success*. Glancing inside, she reads, "Many of our officers handwrite several thousand notes each year. Besides being loving, we know this is meaningful to our People because we hear from them if we miss something significant in their lives like the high school graduation of one of their kids. We just believe in accentuating the positive and celebrating People's successes."[27] "Sounds nice," she mumbles, "but a little too touchy-feely. Let's look for something more down-to-earth."

Continuing her search, she picks up *Power: Why Some People Have It and Others Don't*. She reads, "You can compete and triumph in organizations of all types . . . if you understand the principles of power and are willing to use them. Your task is to know how to prevail in the political battles you will face."[28] She wonders, "Does it really all come down to politics? It seems so cynical and scheming. Isn't there something more uplifting?"

She spots *Tribal Leadership: Leveraging Natural Groups to Build a Thriving Organization*. She ponders its message: "Tribal leaders focus their efforts on building the tribe, or, more precisely, upgrading the tribal culture. If they are successful, the tribe recognizes them as leaders, giving them top effort, cult-like loyalty, and a track record of success."[29] "Fascinating," she concludes, "but this seems a little too primitive for modern organizations."

In her local bookstore, our diligent executive has discovered fragments that we have assembled into a coherent framework. The four distinct metaphors inform the essence of the books she examined: organizations as factories, families, jungles, and temples or carnivals. But she leaves still looking for something more. Some titles felt more compatible with her way of thinking. Others fell outside her comfort zone. She felt forced to choose one, because no single work brought all four together in a coherent way.

Factories

The first book she stumbled on, *How to Measure Anything*, provides counsel on how to think clearly and get the solid information you need to make decisions, extending a long tradition that treats an organization as a factory and the leader as an analyst and engineer. The structural frame, derived from sociology, depicts a world based on reason and emphasizes rationality and structure, including policies, goals, technology, specialized roles, coordination, and formal relationships.

Structures—commonly depicted by organization charts—are designed to fit an organization's environment and technology. Leaders allocate responsibilities ("division of labor"). They then create rules, policies, procedures, systems, and hierarchies to coordinate diverse activities into a unified effort. Problems arise when structure doesn't line up with current circumstances. At that point, some form of reorganization or redesign is needed to remedy the mismatch.

Families

Our executive next encountered *Leading with LUV*, with its focus on caring for people. The human resource perspective, rooted in psychology, sees the leader as servant and catalyst in an organization that is much like an extended family, made up of individuals with needs, feelings, prejudices, skills, and limitations. From a human resource view, the key challenge is achieving alignment between organizations and individuals—finding ways for people to get the job done while feeling good about themselves and their work. Followership and caring are seen as essential complements to leadership.

Jungles

Power: Why Some People Have It and Others Don't is a contemporary application of political science that sees organizations as arenas, contests, or jungles, and leaders as warriors, advocates, and negotiators. Parochial interests compete for power and scarce resources. Conflict is rampant because of enduring differences in interests, perspectives, and resources among contending individuals and groups. Bargaining, negotiation, coercion, and compromise are part of everyday life. Coalitions form around specific interests and change as issues come and go. Problems arise when power is concentrated in the wrong places or is so broadly dispersed that nothing gets done. Solutions arise from a leader's political skill and acumen—as Machiavelli suggested centuries ago in *The Prince*.

Temples and Carnivals

Finally, our executive encountered *Tribal Leadership*, with its emphasis on culture, symbols, and spirit as keys to organizational success. The symbolic lens, drawing on interpretive sociology and cultural anthropology, treats organizations as temples, tribes, theaters, or carnivals, with leaders functioning as magicians, prophets, and poets. It abandons the assumption of rationality prominent in other frames and depicts organizations as cultures propelled by rituals, ceremonies, stories, heroes, and myths rather than by rules, policies, power, and managerial authority. Organizations are also theaters: actors play their roles in the drama while audiences form impressions from what they see on stage. Problems arise when actors play their parts badly, symbols lose their meaning, or ceremonies and rituals lose their potency. Leaders rekindle the expressive or spiritual side of organizations through the use of symbol, myth, and magic.

MULTIFRAME THINKING

The overview of the four-frame model in Exhibit 1.1 shows that each of the frames has its own image of reality. You may be drawn to some and repelled by others, as was our bookstore visitor. Some perspectives may seem clear and straightforward, while others seem puzzling. But learning to apply all four makes you a better, more versatile leader. The evidence is clear that the ability to use multiple frames is associated with greater effectiveness for managers and leaders.[30] Like Lou Gerstner, successful leaders reframe, consciously or intuitively, until they understand the situation at hand. They use multiple perspectives to develop a diagnosis of what's really going on and what course of action might set things right. They transform puzzlement into a comprehensive view of complex situations.

Leaders operate in circumstances that are too complex and messy to take everything in. Consciously or not, they construct simplified cognitive maps in order to make sense of things. The maps are never perfect, but they only need to be good enough for individuals to understand what's going on and what to do next. If your maps are cockeyed, your choices will be too. Your results are disappointing or worse. Our research has repeatedly shown that the odds of success are higher for multiframe leaders who can approach situations from more than one angle. They draw on all four frames to get a more complete picture of any situation.

Less versatile leaders get in trouble because gaps in their thinking keep them from seeing or understanding some of the important challenges they face. They may, for example, be very good at handling technical problems, but mystified by issues of human emotion and motivation. Or they may find conflict so stressful that they can't face political realities. They may trip over subtleties of customs and traditions that they've never learned to see, much less understand.

It all adds up to a simple truth, one that is easy to overlook because it is at odds with everyday experience. The world you perceive is constructed in your mind. Your ideas, or theories, determine whether a given situation is foggy or clear, mildly interesting or momentous, a paralyzing disaster

Exhibit 1.1.
Overview of the Four-Frame Model

	Frame			
	Structural	**Human Resource**	**Political**	**Symbolic**
Metaphor for organization	Factory	Family	Jungle	Temple, theater
Central concepts	Rules, roles, goals, policies, technology, environment	Needs, emotions, skills, relationships	Power, conflict, competition, organizational politics	Culture, meaning, metaphor, ritual, ceremony, stories, heroes
Image of leadership	Social architecture	Empowerment	Advocacy and political savvy	Inspiration, significance
Basic leadership challenge	Attune structure to task, technology, environment	Align organization with human needs and talent	Develop agenda and power base	Create faith, hope, meaning, and belief

or a genuine learning experience. In any situation, there is simply too much happening for you to attend to everything. Your personal theories or frames tell you what is important and what can be safely ignored, and they group scattered bits of information into manageable patterns. Thus it is vital to understand how your habits of mind influence what you see and what you miss or misread.

Multiframe thinking requires moving beyond narrow, mechanical approaches for understanding organizations. We cannot count the number of times managers have told us that they handled some problem the "only way" it could have been. Such statements betray a failure of both imagination and courage and reveal a paralyzing fear of uncertainty. You may find it comforting to think that failure was unavoidable and that you did all you could. But it also can be liberating to realize there is always more than one way to respond to any problem or dilemma. Those who master reframing report a liberating sense of choice, freedom, and power.

Akira Kurosawa's classic film *Rashomon* recounts the same event through the eyes of several witnesses. Each tells a different story. Similarly, every organization is filled with people who have their own interpretations of what is and should be happening. Each version contains a glimmer of truth, but each is a product of the prejudices and blind spots of its maker. No single story is comprehensive enough to make your organization truly understandable or manageable. You need multiple lenses, the skill to use each, and the wisdom to match frames to situations.

CONCLUSION

How leaders think determines what they see, how they act, and what results they achieve. Each of four lenses—structural, human resource, political, and symbolic—opens a new set of possibilities for leaders to use in finding their bearings and choosing a course. Narrow thinking all too often leads to a failure of imagination, a major cause of the shortfall between the reach and the grasp of so many leaders—the empty chasm between noble aspirations and disappointing results. The commission appointed by President George W. Bush to investigate the terrorist attacks of September 11, 2001, concluded that the strikes "should not have come as a surprise" but did because the "most important failure was one of imagination." Multiframe thinking is a powerful stimulus to the broad, creative mind-set that imagination and great leadership require.

See the Appendix for the Leadership Orientations instrument to measure your frame preferences.

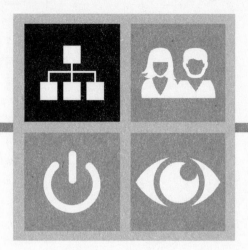

PART 2

Structural Leadership

Structural leaders succeed less through inspiration than through their ability to design a workable social architecture of strategy, roles, and coordination for the times. Great structural leaders share several characteristics:

- They do their homework.
- They insist on clear goals.
- They rethink the relationship of structure, strategy, and environment.
- They focus on detail and implementation.
- They experiment.

Getting Organized

Some leaders pay little attention to structure, either because they don't understand it or because they don't see it as very interesting or important. In Chapter One, when we profiled Lou Gerstner's remarkable turnaround at IBM, we highlighted his symbolic moves to reinvigorate the culture. But it was his strategic and restructuring diligence that initially pulled IBM out of its downward spiral.

Social architecture has been a fundamental underpinning for many other successful leaders, such as McDonald's CEO Jim Skinner, Amazon founder Jeff Bezos, and Xerox CEO Ursula Burns. Using a mantra of "freedom within a framework," Skinner worked to tighten and loosen McDonald's structure at the same time, because he saw the need to respond to two distinct challenges: ensuring that all restaurants conform to McDonald's high standards, while giving units around the world flexibility to adapt to local taste. At Amazon, Bezos delivers customer satisfaction through metrics, technology, and finely tuned systems. Burns reorganized Xerox to merge its historic strengths in technology and hardware with a new push into back-office services. Leaders savvy about structure reason that even in the smallest work situation, people need to know what they're supposed to do, how to work with one another, and who is in charge of what. Otherwise, confusion, finger-pointing, and conflict undermine even the noblest of intentions.

As a leader, you continually choose how to decode the circumstances you face. You can choose to emphasize or ignore structure, to make it central or unimportant. In this chapter, we'll make the case for why structure is essential at the levels of strategic design and execution. We'll start by challenging two common misconceptions: that formal arrangements and bureaucracy are the same, and that there is one best form of social architecture that fits all circumstances. Three cases will help illustrate the two main points. We move to the elements of structure and then to the contingencies, or contextual factors, that determine its contour.

STRUCTURE AT UNITED PARCEL SERVICE (UPS)

Ideas about structure in organization have inherited some misleading baggage. One fallacy is the equating of structure with rigid top-down policies and rules, bureaucracy that impedes work and frustrates workers. In fact, when strategy, rules, policies, control, and measurement are right for an organization's circumstances, people become more productive and satisfied. United Parcel Service provides a familiar example.

The main purpose at UPS—"Big Brown"—is to deliver packages on time to make customers happy. In the early days, UPS delivery workers were "scampering messenger boys"[1] who carried packages to department stores. In recent years, computer technology has replaced employee discretion, and every step from pickup to delivery is highly routinized. Every movement of drivers at UPS is studied, refined, and programmed: "In God we trust; everything else we measure."[2] Detailed instructions specify where and in what order to place packages on delivery trucks. Drivers follow computer-generated routes (which minimize mileage and left turns to save time and gas). The number of steps to your door is premeasured by GPS. If a driver sees you while walking briskly to the door with your parcel, you'll get a friendly greeting. Look carefully and you'll notice that the driver carries an electronic locking device. That's part of the delivery routine: get out of the truck, retrieve package, lock truck, place package in designated place, jauntily return to truck, unlocking door en route. Given that they're on such a tight leash, you might expect demoralized employees. But the technology makes the job more predictable, helps drivers be productive, and keeps customers satisfied. As one driver remarked with a smile, "We're happy robots."

McDONALD'S AND HARVARD: A STRUCTURAL ODD COUPLE

A second misunderstanding about structure is that there is one best way to organize. There is no shortage of consultants hawking proprietary models.

But the most effective social architecture—hierarchy of authority, division of labor, and coordination of work—depends on how leaders assess the situation. Consider two contrasting examples.

McDonald's, the company that made the Big Mac a household word, has been enormously successful. Since Ray Kroc started to take McDonald's across America in the 1950s, the company has become an almost unstoppable growth engine, dominating the worldwide fast-food business. McDonald's has a relatively small staff at its world headquarters near Chicago; most of its employees are salted across the world in more than thirty-one thousand local outlets. Despite its size and geographic reach, McDonald's holds things together in a centralized organization in which most major decisions are made at the top.

Managers and employees of individual restaurants have limited discretion. Much of their work is controlled by technology; machines time french fries and measure soft drinks. The parent company uses powerful systems to ensure that customers get what they expect. A Big Mac tastes about the same whether purchased in New York, Beijing, or Moscow. Guaranteed standard quality inevitably limits the discretion of people who own and work in individual outlets. Cooks are not expected to develop creative new versions of the Big Mac or Quarter Pounder.

All that tight structure might sound oppressive, but a major miscue in the 1990s resulted from trying to loosen up. Responding to pressure from some frustrated franchisees, McDonald's in 1993 stopped sending out inspectors to grade restaurants on service, food, and ambience. When left to police themselves, some restaurants slipped badly. Customers noticed, and the company's image sagged. Ten years later, a new CEO brought the inspectors back to correct lagging standards. But even as it centralized quality control, the company also gave regional managers more leeway to align offerings with their local market in response to globalization and a desire to serve customers better. So a burger will taste pretty much the same wherever you buy it, but you can also get breakfast porridge at McDonald's outlets in England, veggie burgers in India, and burgers-on-wheels home delivery in traffic-choked cities such as Cairo and Taipei.

On the other end of the spectrum, Harvard University is at or near the top of almost every list of the world's best universities. Like McDonald's, it has a small administrative group at the top, but in most other respects, the two organizations diverge dramatically. Harvard is more geographically concentrated than McDonald's, but it is significantly more decentralized. The bulk of Harvard's activities occur within a few square miles of Boston and Cambridge, Massachusetts. Most employees are housed in the university's several schools: Harvard College (the undergraduate school), the graduate faculty of arts and sciences, and various professional schools. Each school has its own dean and its own endowment, and, in accordance with Harvard's philosophy of "every tub on its own bottom," each largely controls its own destiny. Schools have fiscal autonomy, and individual professors have almost unlimited discretion over courses they teach, research they do, and university activities they pursue, if any. Faculty meetings are often sparsely attended. If a dean or a department head wants a faculty member to chair a committee or offer a new course, the request is more often a humble entreaty than an authoritative command.

The contrast between McDonald's and Harvard is particularly strong at the level of service delivery. No one expects individual personality to influence the quality of McDonald's burgers. But everyone expects each Harvard course to be the unique creation of an individual professor. Two schools might offer courses with the same title but different content and widely divergent teaching styles. Efforts to develop standardized core curricula founder on the autonomy of individual professors.

In early 2000, President Larry Summers ran into the predictable challenges of trying to tighten up a professional organization. In attempting to achieve greater control over a fractious faculty, he inadvertently set off one bomb after another. In one case, he suggested that superstar African American studies professor Cornell West redirect his scholarly efforts. Summers gave his advice to West in private, but West's pique soon made the front page of the *New York Times*. Summers's profuse public apologies failed to deter the offended professor from decamping to Princeton. Summers resigned under duress in 2006 after the shortest tenure for a Harvard president since a long-forgotten incumbent died in office in 1862.

The examples of McDonald's and Harvard illustrate the central idea of the structural lens: no organization can perform very well without strategies, roles, relationships, and coordination that are workable and appropriate for its circumstances. The right structure helps ensure that individuals know what they're supposed to do and how they're expected to work with others to get it done.

A basic leadership responsibility is to shape structure to fit the situation. In doing that, leaders always face three key questions: *What are my strategies and circumstances? How do I allocate responsibilities across different people and units? And, once I've done that, how do I integrate diverse efforts in pursuit of common goals?* We'll explore these basic questions and describe options leaders consider when designing an arrangement that will work.

ELEMENTS OF SOCIAL ARCHITECTURE

Every structure is designed and crafted using a particular configuration of basic elements. One is the hierarchy of authority, or chain of command, typically with three levels: executive, managerial, and operational. Authority for making decisions can be concentrated at any of the three levels. A second element is the division of labor. Executives, for example, monitor the environment, set long-range strategy, and keep their eye on the bottom line. Managers set goals and objectives, supervise workers, and check short-term results. Workers at the operational level perform basic tasks.

Managers also have to decide how to group individuals into work units. They can choose among six basic options:

- Functional groups based on *knowledge or skill*, as in the case of a university's academic departments or the classic industrial units of research, engineering, manufacturing, marketing, and finance.

- Units created on the basis of *time*, as by shift (day, swing, or graveyard shifts).

- Groups organized by *product:* detergent versus bar soap, wide-body versus narrow-body aircraft, smartphones versus tablets.

- Groups established around *customers or clients*, as in hospital wards created around patient type (pediatrics, intensive care, or maternity), computer sales departments organized by customer (corporate, government, education, individual), or schools targeting students in particular age groups.

- Groupings around *place or geography*, such as McDonald's retail outlets in different countries or neighborhood schools in different parts of a city.

- Grouping by *process:* a complete flow of work, as with "the order fulfillment process. This process, as in UPS, flows from initiation by a customer order, through the functions, to delivery to the customer."[3]

Once authority is established and roles and responsibilities defined, structural design needs to provide ways to link the parts together. The challenge is to develop an appropriate mix of vertical and lateral coordination.

- Those at higher levels provide vertical coordination by exercising authority, setting policy and strategy, and establishing planning and control systems.

- Lateral coordination happens through a variety of formal and informal roles, meetings, and groups. Individuals in coordinating roles have diplomatic license to span boundaries across specialized groups and areas. Matrix structures cross business and product lines. Digital technology provides rich channels of informal communication.

CONTEXTUAL FACTORS

Tinkering with structural arrangements requires a clear understanding of your situation. In developing the right social architecture to fit specific conditions, every organization needs to respond to basic contextual factors, outlined in Exhibit 2.1.

Size and Age

Young and small organizations often have loose structures and weak systems. McDonald's began as a single hamburger stand in San Bernardino, California, owned and managed by the McDonald brothers. Their stand was phenomenally successful, but the brothers had little interest in expansion. The concept only took off when Ray Kroc arrived on the scene. Kroc had traveled extensively and knew the restaurant business. When he first saw the McDonald's stand, he immediately envisioned a chain of identical

Exhibit 2.1.
Structural Contingencies

Dimension	Structural Implications
Size and age	Organizations become more complex and formal as they get bigger and older.
Core process	Simple, top-down structures work for stable and predictable tasks, but not for more complex and turbulent ones.
Environment	Stable environments reward simpler structures; uncertain, chaotic conditions require a more complex, flexible structure.
Strategy and goals	Top-down structures work better with consistent, well-defined goals; more ambiguous goals and strategies usually work better with more flexible, decentralized structures.
Information technology	Information technology permits flatter, more flexible, and more decentralized structures.
Nature of the workforce	More educated and professional workers need and want greater autonomy and discretion.

restaurants across America. Once Kroc bought franchise rights, he adopted a top-down approach. At the original outlet, the brothers could change the rules whenever they wanted. Under Kroc, restaurant managers' discretion was limited by the rule that every restaurant had to be a clone of the original.[4]

Core Process

Core technologies vary in clarity, predictability, complexity, and effectiveness. Assembling a Big Mac is relatively routine and programmed. The task is clear, most potential problems are known in advance, and the probability of success is high. A tightly scripted, top-down structure is often perfect when the structural design can anticipate almost every major contingency people might encounter.

In contrast, Harvard's two core processes—research and teaching—are complex and unpredictable. Teaching objectives are knotty and amorphous. Unlike hamburger buns, students are active agents. Which teaching strategies best yield desired results is more a matter of faith than of fact. Even if students could be molded predictably, mystery surrounds the knowledge and skills they will need to succeed in life. Harvard's uncertain technologies of teaching and research, dependent on the skills and knowledge of highly educated professionals, are a key source of its loosely coordinated structure.

Strategy and Goals

Across sectors, a major task of leadership is "the determination of long-range goals and objectives of an enterprise and the adoption of courses of action and allocation of resources necessary for carrying out these goals."[5]

A variety of goals is embedded in strategy. In business firms, goals related to profitability, growth, and market share are relatively specific and easy to measure. Goals of educational or human services organizations are typically much more diffuse: "producing educated men and women" or "improving individual well-being," for example. This is another reason why Harvard adopts a more decentralized, loosely integrated system of roles and relationships.

Information Technology

In the 2003 invasion of Iraq, the United States and its allies had an obvious advantage in military hardware. They also had a powerful structural advantage because their superior information technology gave them a much more flexible and decentralized command structure. Commanders in the field could quickly change their plans to respond to new developments. Iraqi forces, meanwhile, had a much slower, more vertical structure that relied on decisions from the top. One reason that Iraqi resistance was lighter than expected in the early weeks was that field commanders waited for instructions that never came because they were cut off from their chain of command.[6]

Later, the structure and technology so effective against Iraq's military had more difficulty with the emerging resistance movement. The Internet and cell phones enabled the resistance to structure itself as a network of loosely connected cells, each pursuing its own agenda in response to local conditions. The absence of strong central control in such networks impedes coordination, but can still be a virtue because local units can adapt very quickly to new developments and because the loss of any one outpost does little damage to the whole.

Nature of the Workforce

Top-down structure works particularly well for jobs that can be programmed in advance, so that workers don't need to make complex, independent judgments in response to changing conditions. There used to be more jobs like that, but the world has been changing, and many lower-level jobs now require higher levels of skill. A better-educated workforce expects and often demands more discretion in daily work routines. Increasing specialization has professionalized many functions. Dramatically different structures are emerging as a result of changes in workforce demographics. These include atomized or networked organizations, made up of small, autonomous, often geographically dispersed work groups tied together by information systems and symbols. Work from home is another example of a trend moving work to where the people are rather than moving people to where the work is.[7]

APPLYING THE STRUCTURAL FRAME

Suppose for the moment that you have become a regional sales manager for an investment bank.[8] You manage a group that sells sophisticated financial instruments (bonds, mortgage-backed securities, options, futures, and so on) to institutional clients such as banks, insurance companies, and pension funds. Your office has been profitable and successful, but the business has become more competitive and complex in recent years. New low-cost competitors are entering the market and siphoning away sales of low-end, simpler products. Your firm is trying to shift its marketing mix to sell more complex products that have less competition and higher profit margins.

Most of your sales are generated by a small group of major account representatives who have the experience, people skills, intellect, and street smarts the work requires. Each of them sells your full line of products to a specific group of a dozen or so big institutional clients. A strong relationship with customers is vital, and each salesperson has a large expense account for entertaining. Top salespeople can make as much as $1 million a year in salary and commissions.

Here's what worries you. As the products keep getting more complicated, it's becoming very hard for your major account representatives and their customers to keep up. Your salespeople can get help from in-house specialists, but when a customer asks about a particular product, the account representative would rather give an answer than say, "I'll have to get back to you on that." Even more important, it's hard to sell what you don't understand, but the most profitable products are the hardest to decode. Market data suggests that competitors are gaining on you because of this expertise gap. What should you do now? Your first thought might be to put in some kind of training or motivational program for the salespeople. Managers often try to fix problems by fixing the people, but miss structural solutions that are more effective and easier to implement. Three simple questions can help guide a structural analysis:

1. What's going on? What's working and not working?

2. What's changing (in your organization, your technology, or your environment) that creates an opportunity, a threat, or both?

3. What problem do you need to solve? What options should you consider?

In this case, your thinking might take you in a direction similar to the following:

1. What's going on?

Start by examining how the job of the account representatives is defined. Consider the options for dividing work (function, time, product, customer, place, process), and you'll see that the role has been defined by customer. All the representatives sell the same products, but each has a unique group of clients. Examine the advantages and disadvantages of this arrangement, and you'll see that it's a good way to create strong relationships between representatives and their clients while giving customers the convenience of one-stop shopping. Whatever question they have or product they want, clients only need contact information for one person. It's a straightforward structure that's easy to understand and reduces the need for coordination among the sales staff.

2. What's changing?

A central idea in the structural frame is that structure needs to align with circumstances. If the environment changes, there's a good chance that the structure has to adapt. The representatives have been generalists who cover the entire product line. That used to work well enough, but it is turning into a liability as the firm tries to shift to more sophisticated products. The representatives can't always answer clients' questions, and may miss opportunities because they don't see the connection between client needs and the more specialized offerings. It's tempting for them to keep selling the simpler, lower-margin products that they understand, but the high end is where competitors have been eating market share.

3. What problem do you need to solve? What options should you consider?

The problem you'd like to solve is that of shifting the sales mix toward more high-margin products. What structural change would help solve that problem? If the goal is to increase the representatives' ability to sell more complex products, a promising fix is to define the representatives' job by product rather than customer. That would let each of the representatives specialize and become an expert on a segment of the product line. But there are trade-offs. Customers might be unhappy because it would make things more complicated; they'd have to contact different people depending on which product they were interested in. Moreover, it's a structure that would require more coordination among the sales representatives in order to keep track of what's happening with each customer. You don't want customers feeling neglected because no one calls or harassed because everyone does. A third risk is that the new structure could fail if the representatives resist it or can't adjust to it.

What to do? The analysis suggests that it makes sense to explore a move from a structure based on the customer to one built around products, but it's not likely to work unless the representatives support the change and work as a team. That suggests involving the representatives in a discussion of how to solve the current problem, knowing that a solution that they believe in has a good chance of working and that the odds are against anything that doesn't make sense to them.

In a real-world case similar to this one, that's basically what happened. The regional sales manager held extensive discussions of the issue with the major account representatives, who eventually agreed to restructure so that each became a specialist in a particular product line. Seeing the importance of working together in this new structure, they defined themselves as the "key account team," with one of their members serving as the coordinator.

After structural change, it is often the case that things get worse before they get better, and that was true in this case. There was short-term confusion as everyone tried to adapt to the new arrangement. Some customers saw the new structure as an improvement; others preferred the old one. Some of the representatives struggled with the transition. The new structure wasn't perfect—no structure is—but six months later, the team was achieving the central goal: profits were up because they were selling more high-margin products to satisfied customers.

CONCLUSION

When leaders neglect structure and strategy, or buy into the two structural fallacies we discussed, they and their organizations pay a price. Units perform far below their potential. They waste time and money on training programs in a vain effort to solve problems that have more to do with social architecture than with people's skills or attitudes. The right social architecture depends on prevailing circumstances and considers an organization's strategies, technology, people, and environment. Understanding the complexity and variety of design possibilities can help you create patterns and prototypes that work for, rather than against, both your people and your purposes.

Ideally, leaders would be fluent and skilled in all four frames, but few of us are perfectly balanced. If structural thinking is one of your strengths, your natural inclinations can make you a valuable contributor in any team or organizational context. You can help diagnose structural gaps or overlaps and suggest ways to fix them. However, devotees of structural thinking often have difficulty seeing and dealing with messier and less rational human, political, and symbolic issues. Structure is important, but it is not the only dimension critical to top performance. Leaders who lean heavily toward structural thinking will typically feel comfortable organizing tight, well-managed teams focused on the task. But leaders need to be aware of the risk of becoming rigid, authoritarian micromanagers. They may have noble intentions and admirable concern for getting the job done, but may overlook human emotions, politics, and the cohesion that comes from cultural bonds rather than structure. We explore these important dimensions of leadership in subsequent chapters. In Chapter Three, we will home in on the structure of teams and small groups. More and more work gets done in such small units. But the call for more leadership talent grows stronger as these teams encounter structural issues that dampen performance.

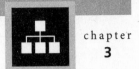
Organizing Groups and Teams

Organizations depend on groups and teams to do much of their work, but teams often founder on structural flaws. A team's structure may come from the top initially, but often needs to evolve locally to meet the challenges of the game, the work at hand. That's where leadership comes in. Whether you're formally in charge or just one of the members, if you're on a team that is going off the rails, there's a leadership opportunity you can seize.

Social architecture is often taken for granted and almost invisible to the members of veteran teams. It is easier for leaders to perceive structural patterns by observing carefully as they emerge in a new team or as changes evolve in an existing one. This chapter begins with two cases of teams in crisis. Together, they illustrate many of the things that can go wrong, including weak leadership, conflict, resistance to authority, lack of accountability, and ball hogging. In one case, the challenges overwhelmed the team's capacities and led to tragedy. In the other, the team, pushed to its limits in a life-and-death test, managed to survive by adapting an idiosyncratic leadership pact. These case stories lead to a discussion of team leadership and the relationship between task and structure. Following this, we explore the task-structure relationship in team sports.

LORD OF THE FLIES

Fiction often illuminates issues that reality obscures. *Lord of the Flies* is a classic novel about a group of boys marooned on a remote island after a plane crash. In the wake of the disaster, the boys were scattered over unknown territory. Two of them came upon a conch shell lying on the beach and found that they were able to summon the others by blowing into the shell.

The boys gathered and decided to elect a leader. Jack, already the official leader of a group of choir boys, proposed himself for the role and was annoyed when the whole group chose Ralph instead. To avoid a divisive struggle, Ralph appointed Jack as the leader of a subgroup charged with killing the plentiful native pigs for food. In a subsequent meeting, Ralph gave everyone a chance to participate in group decisions, declaring that whoever held the conch shell had the floor at communal meetings. With a fragile authority system in place, the group assigned responsibilities for the basic tasks of building shelter, gathering water, and tending the signal fire.

The frail structure soon began to fall apart. Roles and rules were ignored. Duties were neglected. Boys pursued individual interests and took advantage of the freedom to frolic. The neglected signal fire went out, allowing a large ship to pass by without noticing the marooned group. The group split in two. Jack solidified his command of the pig hunters and ruled with an iron hand. His group's hunting activities quickly became a pagan rite, with a pig's head rather than the conch shell as a unifying symbol. Ralph maintained control of his orderly subgroup. He tried to exercise his authority to bring the two groups together, but lacked the clout and command skill to pull it off.

From there, Jack's group spiraled into anarchy, becoming a barbaric band of savages with paint on their faces and pagan ceremonial rites to bond them together, especially after a pig kill. Finally, group members turned on each other in senseless killing. Brute force, mainly wielded by Jack, was the only source of control. When help finally arrived, both the boys and their rescuers were stunned at the striking descent from reason to bedlam.

In the story, we see a structural death spiral. Ralph and Jack were wrapped in a struggle for leadership and unable to establish viable authority. Splintered roles and unheeded rules undermined accountability and reliable performance of essential tasks. In the absence of effective guardrails, the group veered off course. Chaos, divided leadership, and conflict led to tragedy.

Lord of the Flies tells a story of group dynamics that mirrors the reality of many real-life tragedies in which leadership fails, structure fractures, and a group falls apart. Yet failure is not inevitable. In a real-world life-and-death situation that became a major media event, inventive leadership turned potential tragedy into a remarkable story of courage, fortitude, and success.

SAGA OF THE TRAPPED CHILEAN MINERS

A copper mine near Copiapó, Chile, collapsed in August 2010, trapping thirty-three miners 2,300 feet underground in a 549-foot safety shelter. In high humidity and a temperature near ninety degrees, individual miners braced themselves against the hurricane-force winds and eye-clogging dust that often accompany disastrous cave-ins.[1]

As the brutal blasts of air, falling rock, and dust began to subside, Luis Urzúa, the shift foreman, sought to control the panicky men. In a Chilean mine, the foreman is normally the absolute authority, but in the confusion and chaos, he was in danger of losing control. Mario Sepúlveda, the unofficial jester in the group, began to take leadership. Known to the men as *el Perry* (Chilean slang for Good Dude) or *el Loco* (the Crazy One), he began to usurp Urzúa's authority by organizing the men into three separate missions. Each subgroup explored an area of the cave, except for Urzúa, a trained topographer, who began to construct a map of the new surroundings. The only men who did not participate in the explorations were Juan Illanes and four other workers who were outside Urzúa's chain of command and did not acknowledge his or Sepúlveda's leadership.

For one night, anarchy prevailed and the men behaved like a pack of hungry animals, defecating and urinating anywhere and bedding down at random places in the shelter. The next morning, Henriquez, a preacher as well as a miner, called on a higher moral authority to summon the men to a ritual and calm them with prayer. Then Urzúa and Sepúlveda organized a mission to use any available means (dynamite, for example) to communicate to rescuers on the surface that they were still alive. A second group of miners was charged with scouting a possible escape route up one of the ventilator shafts. At the end of the day, a leadership crisis was brewing: Sepúlveda was beginning to take charge.

The next morning, a glimmer of routine and unity was beginning to emerge, and the miners asked to repeat the prayer meeting. Later that afternoon, a conflicted hierarchy began to morph into a democracy. Each man had one vote; ideas were debated and decided on merit instead of the authority of the sponsor. Later that night, struggles over resources again began to divide the men. Humidity and sweat inside the main shelter were so miserable that the men broke into three sleeping groups based on kinship and friendship ties. The two leaders, Urzúa and Sepúlveda, were in a group called "the 105"; another group known as *Refugio* moved into the safety shelter; a third group, left to fend for itself, moved into a dangerous sleeping spot on the mine's main road or ramp. It was called *Rampa*.

After prayers on Day 3, Sepúlveda called a group meeting and rallied the men with his usual enthusiasm. He lectured the group to respect Urzúa but also indicated that he would be willing to take the lead if no one else was ready. As the meeting ended, the men went about their business, settling into roles consistent with their skills. Bustos, a hydraulics engineer, drafted a machinery operator to work on building a series of canals running through the camp to divert water. Pena hooked up a light system rigged to some vehicles trapped in the cave outside the shelter. Illanes, now drawn into the group, used the vehicle batteries to charge headlamps. Zamora, a vehicle mechanic, put his literary talents to work as the group scribe. Urzúa and Sepúlveda, by group vote, controlled access to the meager rations: one-half teaspoon of canned tuna, half the size of a bottle cap, once a day. Mario Gomez, at sixty-three the oldest of the men, became a wise source of optimism. Henriquez, an evangelical preacher, took on the role of *el Pastor*. Barrios, who had learned first aid as a child to help his diabetic mother, became "Dr. House."

As Day 4 arrived, the group's governance and division of labor had solidified except for the tension between Urzúa and Sepúlveda. They had cut the food allotment, but, hungry as they were, waited until all the others had been served before eating. That sense of legitimate order also smoothed what could have become a leadership crisis. Sepúlveda continued to issue orders, allocate tasks, and inspire the men. But he, along with the other men, accorded Urzúa great respect as a shift leader who, in miner's lore, is "sacred and holy" and could not be replaced.[2]

Unity solidified, and the dual leadership of Urzúa and Sepúlveda stabilized. As Day 15 dawned, the men were down to the last of their meager rations. But the sound of drills from the rescue effort on the ground kept hope alive, until the closest drill missed. As faith began to wane, Henriquez again assumed his pastoral role. He summoned the men and asked them to put their hands on the food box and pray to God to duplicate the last two cans of tuna. That resurrected hope for a while, but the miners were falling into a death spiral as their health deteriorated rapidly. Men who could no longer walk to the primitive toilet spent time writing good-bye letters to family and friends. These final steps toward death continued into Day 16, while rescuers above accelerated their drilling efforts. A drill finally broke through on Day 17. The miners somehow found energy for a jubilant celebration. They painted the drill head with orange spray paint and attached a note: "*Estamos Bien En El Refugio los 33*" (We're OK in the refuge—the 33).When the drill made its way to the surface, it received a thunderous welcome from rescuers, family, and friends.

That marked the end of the first chapter in what would become the longest period anyone had ever survived underground. All the men eventually came out alive. Their structure had continued to evolve, but remained intact until the group was finally rescued. The last squabble came at the end—who would be the last man to leave the mine? Hierarchy and tradition prevailed. Urzúa got the honor and emerged last, receiving the acclaim of spectators and media and claiming the record for the person buried underground longest and surviving.

COMPARING LEADERSHIP DYNAMICS

Both groups, boys and miners, struggled with the gravity of their situations, moving from chaos to a nascent form of democracy. In the case of the stranded boys, the one person–one vote agreement yielded a leader, Ralph, who assigned people to roles. The assignments fell apart from lack of coordination and supervision. Jack challenged Ralph's authority, and in the ensuing leadership struggle, pulled his pack from the group.

The resulting anarchy and unchecked conflict between two warring sub-groups led to the group's descent into chaos and killing.

The miners' experience began much like that of the marooned boys: chaos in the aftermath of disaster, emergence of democracy, and a struggle for leadership between Urzúa and Sepúlveda. But there were significant differences that favored the miners. Urzúa's role as foreman gave him legitimate and traditional authority that the boys' group lacked. But authority is not the same thing as leadership, particularly in a time of crisis. Sepúlveda had a special emotional attachment with the men, and his initiatives filled a leadership vacuum, but he was careful to respect Urzúa's formal authority. Early on, Henriquez (*el Pastor*) assembled the miners for a spiritual meeting, calling on faith in a higher authority to stabilize a volatile situation. His prayers helped calm the miners, and they called on him periodically during their time underground. Urzúa and Sepúlveda managed to agree on a workable way to share leadership. Urzúa would continue as the formal leader while Sepúlveda served as a sort of sly socioemotional cheerleader. Their roles overlapped, and the other men willingly took orders from both.

The early democracy, the invocation of a higher spiritual authority, and the resolution of the contest for leadership calmed the men and readied them for work. As the miners took on responsibilities based on their individual skills, roles emerged rather than being assigned. Urzúa and Sepúlveda supervised and took control of rationing food and responding to other existence concerns. Through various vicissitudes, this basic structure survived until Urzúa ascended from the mine.

The marooned boys began with good intentions. They tried to establish a workable structure, but lacked the miners' advantages in terms of an established authority structure and experience working together as a team. Even with those advantages, the miners struggled to evolve a social architecture that would sustain them. They muddled their way to a viable arrangement: a unique hierarchy of authority, division of labor from the ground up, and workable lateral and vertical coordination. Rationality and commitment to a shared purpose helped the miners survive.

Leadership needs to step up when a team is failing. If the designated boss doesn't have the savvy and skill to get the group back on track, someone else needs to provide the leadership the group needs. Whether they are formal or emergent, structural leaders have a better chance of success if they recognize that the right structure depends on the group's circumstances—what game the team is playing.

TASK AND STRUCTURE IN TEAMS

In developing a team structure, a basic consideration is the nature of the work to be accomplished. Tasks vary in clarity, predictability, and stability. Simple tasks align well with basic structures—clearly defined roles, elementary forms of interdependence, and coordination by plan or command. More complicated projects generally require more complex structure: flexible roles, mutual give-and-take, and harmonization through lateral dealings and communal feedback. But when a situation becomes exceptionally ambiguous and fast paced, particularly when time pressure is high, reverting to more centralized authority often works best. Otherwise, groups may not make decisions quickly enough. Without a structure aligned to the work, performance and morale suffer, and troubles multiply.

We have looked at two teams—boys and miners—that needed to change their structure to meet new challenges. One succeeded; the other did not. In ongoing teams, it is often the case that the team needs to vary its structure to meet the requirements of different tasks. An example is a U.S. Army commando team that compiled a distinctive record in World War II. It accomplished every mission, including extremely high-risk operations, with remarkably few soldiers wounded or killed. A research team concluded that the unit's success was not a matter of unusually high training or talent. Instead, the group was very good at reconfiguring its structure to fit the situation. When planning in advance of missions, the group functioned much like a town meeting. Anyone could volunteer ideas and make suggestions. Decisions were reached by consensus, and the engagement strategy was approved by the group as a whole. The unit's planning structure resembled that of an R&D team or a creative design group. Battle plans reflected the group's best ideas.

When it came time to execute, the group's structure transformed from a loose, creative confederation to a tightly controlled chain of command. Every individual had specific assignments. Tasks had to be done with split-second precision. The team's leader had sole authority for making operational decisions or revising the plan. Everyone else obeyed orders without question, though they could offer suggestions if time permitted. In battle, the group relied on the traditional military structure: clear-cut responsibilities and decisions were made at the top. The group's ability to tailor its structure captured the best of two worlds. Participation encouraged creativity, ownership, and understanding of the battle plan. Authority, accountability, and clarity enabled the group to function with speed and efficiency in combat.

STRUCTURES OF SPORTS TEAMS

The structural possibilities in teams are almost endless, but the options generally fall into one of several recognizable patterns. Team sports, among the most popular pastimes around the world, offer a helpful way to cut through the complexity and clarify how structure varies depending on the task. Because every competition calls for its own unique patterns of interaction, different sports call for different arrangements of people. Social architecture is thus remarkably different for baseball, football, and basketball. So is the nature of leadership. Defining the game is a prerequisite to building your team.

Sum of the Parts: Baseball

As baseball player Pete Rose once noted, "Baseball is a team game, but nine men who meet their individual goals make a nice team."[3] In baseball, as in cricket and other bat-and-ball games, a team is a loosely integrated confederacy. Individual efforts are mostly independent, seldom involving more than two or three players at a time. Particularly on defense, players are separated from one another by significant distance. The loose connections reduce the need for synchronization among the various positions. The pitcher and catcher must each know what the other is going to do, and, at times, infielders must anticipate how a teammate will act. But a hitter is alone in the batter's box, and a center fielder is alone in a large expanse. Managers' decisions are mostly tactical, normally involving individual substitutions or actions. They typically stand in the dugout, wearing the team uniform, ostensibly thinking strategically. Managers can come and go without seriously disrupting a team's play. Players can transfer from one team to another with relative ease, because a newcomer can do the job without major disruption to a team's style of play. John Updike summed it up well: "Of all the team sports, baseball, with its graceful intermittence of action, its immense and tranquil field sparsely salted with poised men in white, its dispassionate mathematics, seemed to be best suited to accommodate, and be ornamented by, a loner. It is an essentially lonely game."[4]

This kind of structure works whenever it's the case that "if we each do our own job, we'll be fine." An example in a very different context is the structural evolution of Al-Qaeda. It began in Afghanistan in the 1980s as a centralized, top-down organization under the leadership of Osama bin Laden. Expelled from its safe haven and seriously damaged by the U.S. invasion of Afghanistan, it adapted to circumstances and evolved a structure based on local cells that operate independently. Two different cells could be working toward the same mission without knowing it. When not activated for a specified mission, members of these sleeper cells blend with the general populace. As in baseball, the leader's job is to plan tactics and ensure that each separate unit knows its job and has the skills and resources it needs for success. This hydralike team structure looms as a deadly threat that is difficult to combat with traditional command-and-control strategies, and the loss of any one cell does little damage to the whole organization.

Planning the Next Move: Football

American football and other chesslike sports, such as curling, require a structural configuration very different from baseball. These games proceed through a series of moves, or plays. Between plays, teams have time to plan strategy for the next move. In contrast to baseball, football players perform in close proximity. Linemen and offensive backs hear, see, and often touch one another. Each play involves every player on the field. Efforts are sequentially linked in a prearranged plan. The actions of linemen pave the way for the movement of backs; a defensive team's field position becomes the starting point for the offense, and vice versa. In the transition from offense to defense, specialty platoons play a pivotal role. The efforts of individual players are tightly coordinated. George Allen, former coach of the Washington Redskins, put it this way: "A football team is a lot like a machine. It's made up of parts. If one part doesn't work, one player pulling against you and not doing his job, the whole machine fails."[5]

Because of the tight connections among parts, a football team must be well integrated, mainly through planning and top-down control. The primary units are the offensive, defensive, and specialty platoons. Each has its own leader-coordinator. Under the overall leadership of the head coach, the team uses scouting reports and other surveillance to develop a strategy or game plan in advance. During the game, strategic decisions are typically made by the head coach. Tactical decisions are delegated to coordinators or to designated players on offense or defense. Each head coach stands on the sidelines in his unique game-day regalia, surrounded by players and other coaches.

A football team's tight-knit character makes it tougher to swap players from one team to another. Irv Cross, of the Philadelphia Eagles, once remarked, "An Eagles player could never make an easy transition to the Dallas Cowboys; the system and philosophies are just too different."[6] Unlike baseball, football requires intricate strategy and tightly meshed leadership and execution.

Coordination on the Fly: Basketball

Basketball (as well as similar games like soccer, hockey, and lacrosse) requires tight coordination as in football, but in a much more fluid game. In quick, rapidly moving transitions, offense becomes defense—with the same players. The efforts of individuals are highly reciprocal; each player depends on the performance of others. Anyone can handle the ball or try to score.

Basketball is much like improvisational jazz. Teams require a high level of spontaneous, mutual adjustment. Everyone is on the move, often in an emerging pattern rather than a predetermined course. A successful basketball season depends heavily on a flowing relationship among team members who read and anticipate one another's moves. Players who play together over time develop a sense of what their teammates will do. A team of newcomers experiences difficulty in adjusting to individual predispositions or quirks. Keidel notes that coaches, who sit or roam the sidelines, serve as integrators.[7] They are typically dressed in business suits or sport coats. Some are screamers and "towel-wringers"; others (like Phil Jackson) are more contained and stoic. Their periodic verbal or sign-language interventions reinforce team cohesion, helping players coordinate laterally while on the move. Unlike baseball teams, basketball teams are doomed if they play as a collection of individual stars. Unlike football, basketball has no platoons, and the action doesn't stop between plays. It is wholly a harmonized group effort.

A study of Duke University's successful women's basketball team in 2000 documented the importance of group interdependence and cohesion. The team won because players could anticipate the actions of others. The individual "I" deferred to the collective "we." Passing to a teammate was valued as highly as making the shot. Basketball is "fast, physically close, and crowded, 20 arms and legs in motion, up, down, across, in the air. The better the team, the more precise the passing into lanes that appear blocked with bodies."[8]

■ ■ ■

Whenever a new team forms or an old team underperforms, examine the team's task and structure. If you try to play baseball with a structure better adapted to basketball, members will waste time in unnecessary meetings and become frustrated as they trip over one another. Conversely, if the team uses a baseball structure to play basketball, lack of teamwork will doom its efforts, and the whole will be much less than the sum of the parts.

Leadership becomes even more critical in self-managing teams, which many see as the structure of the future. Such teams plan, assign tasks and roles, schedule, make decisions, and solve problems on their own. The model is becoming more and more common as experience and research both suggest that self-directed teams often produce better results and higher morale than groups operating under more traditional top-down control.[9] But *Lord of the Flies* reminds us that there is an important difference between "self-managing" and "leaderless." Self-managing teams usually need help getting started, and work best when they have a clear sense of what game they're playing and how success is defined. More and more well-known firms—such as Microsoft, Boeing, Google, W. L. Gore, Southwest Airlines, Harley-Davidson, and Whole Foods—capitalize on the benefits of self-directed teams. A workable structure helps ensure that these positive paybacks will be realized, and structurally attuned leaders are needed to make sure a team is aligned to compete in its game.

CONCLUSION

A designated leader is no guarantee that a team will be well led. An effective team requires leadership that aligns the group's structure with the group's tasks and circumstances. If the official leader doesn't bring the structural awareness or leadership skills that the team calls for, someone else must step in to ensure that the team stays on track and gets where it needs to go. Structural leaders help groups get clear about why they're there, who is in charge, who is supposed to do what, and how team members can work with one another to achieve the group's purpose. When authority is challenged, they find ways to share leadership so that team members can work together instead of letting conflict undermine team performance.

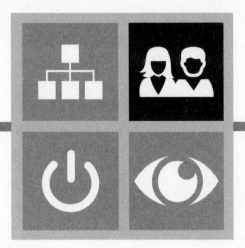

PART 3

Human Resource Leadership

G reat human resource leaders see people as the key to success. They apply a consistent set of people-friendly principles:

- They communicate a strong belief in people.
- They develop a philosophy and practices to put their belief in action.
- They're visible and accessible.
- They empower others.

Leading People

NPR host Adam Davidson and his wife went furniture shopping in 2008 at the Ikea hyperstore in Brooklyn, New York. They hated it. It was an enormous, confusing labyrinth, and they couldn't get any help finding their way around. Angry and frustrated, they vowed never to return. Five years later, the couple relented and gave Ikea a second chance. They were startled at the difference: help was readily available from pleasant, knowledgeable staff. What happened? Ikea had reframed by adopting a new approach to managing people.

Much of the business world views frontline workers as a necessary evil, a cost to be minimized by keeping head count and wages as low as possible. But retailers such as Costco, Trader Joe's, Wegman's, and Mercadona in Spain have found that they get much better results by investing in people. "Costco pays its workers about $21 an hour; Wal-Mart is just about $13. Yet Costco's stock performance has thoroughly walloped Wal-Mart's for a decade."[1]

Structural thinking and leadership are powerful and vital, but by themselves they are rarely enough. Legions of managers have built a career or a business using structural thinking, only to crash into the limits of a single frame. Their career stalls, or their business goes downhill. They work even harder and do even more of what worked in the past, but they no longer get the results they seek. They wonder what's gone wrong and why success is eluding them. Learning to understand people as well as structure would expand their leadership options and improve the odds of success.

These ideas are not new. In the early nineteenth century, a Scotsman, Robert Owen, made a fortune in the textile business by providing better wages and working conditions. He took children off the factory floor and put them in school. He was criticized as a wild radical who would harm the people he hoped to help. A century later, when Henry Ford announced in 1914 that he was going to shorten the workday to eight hours and double the wages of his blue-collar workers from $2.50 to $5.00 per day, he came under heavy criticism from the business community. The *Wall Street Journal* opined that he was "committing economic blunders, if not crimes."[2] The *Journal* got it wrong. Ford's profits doubled over the next two years as productivity soared and employee turnover plunged. Ford later said that the $5 per day was the best cost-cutting move he ever made.[3]

Fast-forward another century to Jim Sinegal, cofounder and longtime CEO of retail giant Costco. He put in place many of the structural elements that fueled Costco's growth, but insisted that treating people well was at the heart of the company's success. Wall Street analysts sometimes complained that he cheated shareholders by charging customers too little and paying employees too much. An unfazed Sinegal replied wryly, "You have to take the shit with the sugar."[4] He could afford to stick to his beliefs—his company was more successful and profitable than competitors who hewed more closely to the analysts' advice.

Organizations need people for their energy, effort, and talent. Individuals need organizations for the many rewards they offer. But the needs of the individual and the organization don't always line up very well. When the fit between people and organizations is poor, one or both suffer. Individuals may feel underpaid, unappreciated, or disrespected. Organizations sputter because individuals give less than their best or work against organizational purposes. Douglas McGregor argued some fifty years ago that the central task of leadership is to ensure alignment between people and organizations so that individuals find satisfying, meaningful work, and organizations get the talent and energy they need to succeed.[5]

In this chapter, we contrast traditional treat-'em-like-dirt strategies with more enlightened approaches for managing people. We'll dig into a story of a company in Brazil that dramatically demonstrates the benefits of creative and progressive strategies for managing people. Then we'll transition to a well-known American clothing retailer, Men's Wearhouse, to see how an enlightened approach to people management can build a remarkably successful business in a tough environment.

TREAT 'EM LIKE DIRT

For most of management history, standard practice has been to treat employees like pawns to be moved where needed and sacrificed when necessary. As one former plant manager put it, "The way you treat people would be awful. You know, the people, they're nothin', they're just a number. You move 'em in and out. If they don't do the job, you fire 'em. If they get hurt, or complain about safety, you put a 'bulls-eye' on them. They're not gonna have a job in the near future."[6]

That attitude explains why so much of the public thinks of bosses as selfish, heartless tyrants. In an era of high unemployment and economic distress, elites in every sector are suspect, and the idea of sacrificing people for profits persists as a popular view of the workplace. One of America's favorite cartoon strips is *Dilbert*, whose white-collar, cubicle-bound hero wanders mindlessly through an office landscape of bureaucratic inertia, corporate doublespeak, and callous, incompetent bosses. The popularity of such images tells us that organizations often manage people badly. They turn employees into sullen, undermotivated loafers or rebels who couldn't care less about the quantity or the quality of what they produce. The human resource frame offers a much more positive and productive way to think about people.

SEMCO: INVESTING IN PEOPLE

A father-son tale from Brazil tells of a young chief executive who shifted from structural to human resource beliefs, saving his health and his company's future in the process. The father, Curt Semler, was born in Austria in 1912 and trained as an engineer before he moved to Brazil in the 1950s. There he built Semco, a successful manufacturing business. The elder Semler ran his company like a good Austrian engineer—with a strong emphasis on efficiency, command, and control. By 1982, he faced a painful dilemma. Sales had plummeted, and the business was struggling amid a downturn in the Brazilian economy.

Semler's dream was to leave his business to his only son, Ricardo. So he brought Ricardo into the company and put him in an adjacent office. Ricardo was smart, educated, and hard working and, to his father's relief, had given up his dream of becoming a rock guitarist. But Ricardo was still young and rebellious, and he chafed under his father's tight leash. The two of them fought constantly, and Ricardo finally said he'd had enough—he was going to quit Semco and go off on his own.

So what do you do if you're the elder Semler? Do you wish your son well as he storms out the door? Or do the one thing that might convince him to stay: turn your business over to a twenty-four-year-old with little management experience who will probably take the business in some wild new directions? Faced with those painful options, Curt Semler reluctantly turned over control of the business to Ricardo, telling him: "Better make your mistakes while I'm still alive." What followed was one of the more surprising and dramatic stories in business history.

Young, inexperienced, and fearless, Ricardo grabbed the reins with gusto. Working feverishly, he fired most of his father's top managers, diversified into new businesses, and pulled the company out of a cash crunch. His first moves were structural. He installed elaborate information and control systems and brought in tough executives to enforce them. It worked—to a point. The business results improved, but at a personal cost: Ricardo was killing himself. His many health issues included fainting spells, gastritis, skin rashes, and a chronic sore throat. When a doctor told him that he was physically fine but his stress levels were off the charts, Ricardo decided he had to change his lifestyle.

Until then, Ricardo had retained and reinforced much of the top-down, bureaucratic approach developed on his father's watch. Now he looked for ways to work less and delegate more. He read books, consulted peers, and experimented with assorted management fads of the time. Nothing seemed to help, but he kept looking. The company seemed to be well organized and disciplined, but he wasn't getting the performance he wanted, and Semco did not feel like a happy place. He decided to go for broke, launching his company on a high-risk journey into the unknown. Along this new path, Ricardo and his company rediscovered and adapted many of the principles for leading people used by progressive leaders and organizations around the globe (summarized in Exhibit 4.1). Much of what he tried was not new, but few companies had gone as far—or as fast.

Exhibit 4.1.
Principles for Leading People

Human Resource Principle	Semco's Approach
Develop a philosophy and values	Experiment and learn from experience
	Instill values of trust, transparency, and democracy
Hire the right people	Know what you want
	Be selective
Keep them around	Promote from within
	Protect jobs
	Share the wealth
Invest in their future	Provide learning opportunities
	Rotate jobs
Sustain power to the people	Open the books
	Foster egalitarianism
	Encourage self-managing teams and business units
	Redesign work
	Make decisions democratically
Promote diversity	Initiate Semco's Woman project

Developing a Philosophy and Values

When Ricardo began his quest, he had no idea where he was going or how he would eventually get there. He embarked on a series of experiments and gradually homed in on three key values—trust, transparency, and democracy. These sound simple enough, but Semco took them to heart, with dramatic results.

Trust was a central theme when Ricardo decided to eliminate some of the most "visible signs of corporate oppression."[7] His first step was simple: ending the standard practice of searching employees as they left the plant. Managers objected: frisking workers was the only way to prevent theft. The union complained: searches were the workers' best defense against false accusations. Despite the opposition, Ricardo replaced searches with signs politely asking workers not to exit with anything that didn't belong to them. To Ricardo, whether theft decreased or not really didn't matter. He wanted employees to get the message, "We trust you."

Over time, Ricardo evolved an unorthodox philosophy of management:[8]

> The key to management is to get rid of all the managers.
> The key to getting work done on time is to stop wearing a watch.
> The best way to invest corporate profits is to give them to the employees.
> The purpose of work is not to make money. The purpose of work is to make the employees, whether working stiffs or top executives, feel good about life.

Hiring the Right People

In studying Semco managers who failed, Ricardo realized that they often were technically capable but lacking in leadership talent. In response, he developed a system in which subordinates rated their bosses on both technical ability *and* leadership. Those with low scores either improved or were fired. Ricardo applied the same approach to hiring new managers. People who would be working with a new manager made the hiring decision, using ratings of both technical qualifications and leadership. Job applicants went through multiple rounds of interviews, fully aware that their fate depended on the judgments of their prospective colleagues and subordinates. The process was grueling, but it helped ensure that new hires fit with Semco's distinctive ways and enjoyed the support of their new colleagues.

Keeping Them

To attract the right people, progressive companies reward generously and share the business profits. To retain loyal and hardworking employees, they protect jobs and promote from within. Semco shared the wealth through an employee-driven profit-sharing system. The company put about a quarter of its profits into a profit-sharing pool, and workers hammered out a process for distribution. Each unit got a share based on its profits for the year, and everyone in the unit got the same amount.

One of Semco's compensation experiments was "name your price," allowing people to set their own pay. The company gave people data about what they could make elsewhere and what Semco paid for similar jobs in the company. Many observers might wonder: Why wouldn't people ask for more than they were worth? Because at Semco, colleagues would notice, and "gougers" would price themselves out of a job.

Semco also kept retention rates high by promoting from within and protecting jobs. In some jobs and industries, turnover can run over 100 percent a year. This gets expensive because of the high cost of hiring and training replacements and because newcomers are prone to confusion and error. Semco rarely fires people, and annual turnover is less than 1 percent.[9] The company posts open positions internally and gives first preference to current employees. The company searches outside only if no qualified insider applies. When it faces downturns, Semco has asked employees to look for creative alternatives to layoffs. During one sustained economic slump, workers voted to close a plant, over the management's objections. Executives wanted to avoid layoffs, but the workers had studied the numbers and concluded that Semco couldn't afford to keep the plant open. When Semco did lay off workers, the company had a program to help them start businesses selling goods or services to Semco or other customers. White- and blue-collar workers formed more than two dozen companies providing everything from legal services to software to contract manufacturing.

Investing in People

Organizations are sometimes reluctant to invest in developing their human capital. The costs of training are immediate and easy to measure, whereas the benefits are more elusive and long term. Semco understands that undertrained workers cause harm by delivering shoddy quality, poor service, and costly mistakes.

The company invests in employees in a variety of creative ways. One is a job rotation program in which about 20 to 25 percent of managers change jobs in any given year. Another program, called "Lost in Space," allows young recruits to meander around the company for a year, working in any job or unit that interests them. At the end of the year, any unit can offer them a job. Another program, "Rush Hour MBA," offered classes at 6 P.M. so that employees could take a class instead of battling the rush-hour crush. After class, they could enjoy a more relaxed drive home.

Sustaining Power to the People

Empowerment has become another management buzzword. Like many other corporate shibboleths, it's easier to preach than practice. At Semco, empowerment is fundamental to the company's approach to managing people. Democracy is a central theme at Semco. It began with symbolic changes—eliminating the dress code, democratizing the parking lot, closing executive dining rooms, and eliminating private offices. Secretaries and receptionists were moved to other jobs, and managers learned to make copies and answer their own phones. Gone were all the old status markers—how people dressed, how far they had to walk to their car, where they ate, or the size of their office.

Semco also embraced a philosophy known as "open-book management" that has taken root in a number of progressive companies. The books were open to all employees, and training in financial literacy helped them make sense of the numbers. This approach was another clear signal that management trusted people, and it gave employees a powerful incentive to contribute. They could see how their work affected the bottom line and how the bottom line affected them.

Over time, the company took democratic decision making to a level few companies have ever contemplated. Workers began to design production processes and products, approve or veto new businesses, set production quotas, and set their own hours and pay. They elected and evaluated their bosses. For big decisions, everyone got a vote.

The basic organizational units at Semco are small, self-managing groups of roughly six to ten people. These teams are typically grouped in business units of no more than a few hundred people. Ricardo's theory holds that you can minimize rules and bureaucracy if you keep things small and simple. When groups face a new opportunity or challenge, they start talking about how to handle it among themselves.

Promoting Diversity

Believing that companies have a responsibility to combat discrimination, the company initiated policies and projects to promote fairness. One was

"Semco Woman," which began when the company encouraged groups of women at every level to meet and discuss shared concerns. The women started with a push for better locker rooms and office bathrooms, but then moved on to bigger issues such as day care and career opportunities.

MEN'S WEARHOUSE: GETTING IT RIGHT

Your circumstances may not be the same as Ricardo Semler's, and not all the specifics in his playbook will be right for your situation. You'll need to experiment and learn from experience, just as he did. But Semler's example shows that following a broad set of principles for managing people, combined with courage and creativity, can produce extraordinary results. Ricardo is not alone. Many other leaders have built teams of talented, loyal, and free-spirited people who will go out of their way to get the job done. Such employees are less likely to make costly blunders or to jump ship as soon as someone offers them a better deal. That's a potent edge—in sports, business, or anywhere else.

The Semco case offers a toolbox of ideas for thinking from a human resource angle. To test your ability to apply these ideas, imagine yourself in the situation of another successful business leader. Suppose that after college, you spent a few years selling men's clothing and discovered that it was fun and you were good at it. You feel you're ready for the next challenge—launching your own business. You'll begin with a single store, but you hope to get larger over time. You know you'll be entering a tough industry with slow growth and lots of competition. So how do you stand out in a crowded, competitive field? One thing you know is that your competitors' employees typically live with low pay and mediocre management. Maybe if you treat your people better, they'll make your customers happier.

How might you do that? You could ask yourself the questions we discussed in the Semco case:

1. What philosophy and values will you follow?

2. What will you look for in the people you hire?

3. How will you keep people once they sign on?

4. What will you do to invest in your people?

5. How will you empower your people?

6. How will you promote diversity?

George Zimmer developed answers to those questions that worked for him. He founded Men's Wearhouse in 1973, when he was twenty-four years old. He began with a single store, but a quarter-century later, the company had grown to more than a thousand outlets generating close to $2 billion in revenue, even as the men's suit business went downhill and many competitors went out of business. You've probably seen Zimmer in one of his many television commercials with his signature line, "You're going to like the way you look—I guarantee it."

Our list of key practices for leading people provides a quick guide to Zimmer's road map for success:

1. Develop a philosophy and values

Zimmer was clear and succinct about his company's basic philosophy and values: "We're not in the suit business, we're in the people business . . . There has to be a democratization of everything—of effort and the fruits of those efforts. We're always looking for ways here to share the wealth and really make it win-win."[10]

2. Hire the right people

Hiring at Men's Wearhouse was more centralized than at Semco—it was a major responsibility of regional managers—but the company knew what it valued. Competitors often looked for retail experience, but Men's Wearhouse wanted people skills and positive attitude. The company figured that changing personality is hard, but training people to sell suits is easier.

3. Keep them

Turnover at Men's Wearhouse is low by industry standards: 10 percent annually for store managers, compared to 25 percent for the industry.[11] Men's Wearhouse promotes almost entirely from within, and many of the senior executives worked their way up from the sales floor. Firing is centralized, and before letting someone go, the company typically moves the individual to another store or job to offer another chance for success. An employee stock ownership plan gives just about everyone a stake in the company, and store employees are eligible for monthly bonuses based on a store's performance.

4. Invest in them

Men's Wearhouse emphasizes coaching and training, mostly conducted by line managers. New sales staff spend a week in California at "Suits University," where they learn about selling, the product line, and the company's values and mission. Executives at every level from the CEO down are expected to spend time in stores coaching and selling.

5. Empower them

A central element of the Men's Wearhouse philosophy is to hire "wardrobe consultants," not sales clerks. The consultant's job is not simply to sell what's in the store but to understand what the customer is looking for, ask about his existing wardrobe, and help him meet his work and lifestyle needs. The goal is to provide a positive experience and build a long-term relationship with the customer. Managers are told that their number-one customer is the people who work for them and that their job is to provide staff with the tools and resources they need. Men's Wearhouse also encourages self-expression and having fun; it has built a reputation for great holiday parties.

6. Promote diversity

A long-term commitment to diversity has produced a workforce at Men's Wearhouse that is about half female and more than half minority. In *Fortune*'s 2013 list of America's one hundred best places to work, Men's Wearhouse ranked seventh in terms of workforce diversity.[12]

In 2011, Zimmer turned the reins over to his chosen successor, Doug Ewert, but after a while the two drifted apart. Zimmer began to worry that the new leadership was departing from the people-first philosophy that made Men's Wearhouse successful. He criticized increases in executive compensation that violated his egalitarian credo. All that set the stage for the surprising news in mid-2013 that Zimmer had been fired as both executive chairman and TV pitchman for Men's Wearhouse. The board felt that they had a two-boss problem because Zimmer had not accepted "the fact that Men's Wearhouse is a public company with an independent board of directors and that he [is no longer] the chief executive officer."[13] Did this embarrassing public spat mean that Men's Wearhouse was moving away from the philosophy on which Zimmer built it? Or just that Zimmer was stronger on people leadership than political savvy? Many leaders have paid a price for just that reason.

CONCLUSION

The human resource frame expands leaders' thinking beyond the rational nuts and bolts of narrow structural thinking to an understanding of how to create conditions that foster high levels of motivation, energy, and effort. Leaders who commit themselves to key practices of effective people leadership—developing a philosophy for managing people, hiring the right people, keeping employees and investing in their future, empowering them, and promoting diversity—have repeatedly built businesses that thrive on the strength of employee talent, energy, and creativity.

All would be well if leaders understood themselves and others. Unfortunately, that's not always the case. In Chapter Five, we will examine the roots of interpersonal incompetence among leaders and offer ideas for how they can become better communicators.

Seeing Ourselves as Others See Us

O ne of the most basic and pervasive causes of leadership failure is interpersonal blindness. Many leaders simply don't know their impact on other people. Even worse, they don't know that they don't know. They assume that other people see them pretty much the way they see themselves, then they blame others when things go wrong. A famous example occurred during the 2008 U.S. presidential campaign, after the Republican nominee, John McCain, selected the then largely unknown governor of Alaska, Sarah Palin, to be his running mate. At first, this looked like a smart move, as Palin gave a rousing and well-received acceptance speech at the Republican convention. But Palin was new to the national political scene and lacked familiarity with many of the issues in the campaign. This sometimes got her in trouble when she had to work without a script. A legendary example was an interview on national television with anchor Katie Couric:

> *Couric:* You've cited Alaska's proximity to Russia as part of your foreign policy experience. What did you mean by that?
>
> *Palin:* That Alaska has a very narrow maritime border between a foreign country, Russia, and on our other side, the land—boundary that we have with—Canada. It—it's funny that a comment like that was—kind of made to— cari—I don't know, you know? Reporters—

Couric:	Mock?
Palin:	Yeah, mocked, I guess that's the word, yeah.
Couric:	Explain to me why that enhances your foreign policy credentials.
Palin:	Well, it certainly does because our—our next-door neighbors are foreign countries. They're in the state that I am the executive of. And there in Russia—
Couric:	Have you ever been involved with any negotiations, for example, with the Russians?
Palin:	We have trade missions back and forth. We—we do—it's very important when you consider even national security issues with Russia as Putin rears his head and comes into the air space of the United States of America, where—where do they go? It's Alaska. It's just right over the border. It is—from Alaska that we send those out to make sure that an eye is being kept on this very powerful nation, Russia, because they are right there. They are right next to—to our state.

The interview went viral in the media and on the Internet, and much of the commentary focused on Palin's lack of foreign policy depth. But note Palin's genuine puzzlement about the response she got. "It—it's funny that a comment like that was—kind of made to—cari—I don't know, you know? Reporters—." Palin's comments made sense to her, so she figured there must be something wrong with her critics, those liberal reporters from the "lamestream media" who were out to get her.

Palin is not alone. She provides only one of countless examples of a lack of self-awareness that chronically bedevils leaders, whether on the world stage or in much more mundane situations. A routine example is a boss, B, who thinks he's coaching a subordinate, S, whereas S thinks B is constantly micromanaging. Over time, the boss gets more and more disappointed because S doesn't respond as enthusiastically as he expects. He wonders why S doesn't want to learn and can't follow simple instructions. Meanwhile, S becomes more and more frustrated with a boss who constantly interferes, gives dumb orders, and makes it harder for her to do her job. Because the boss has no clue about the gap between how he sees himself and how S sees him, his efforts to coach just make things worse. Why are gaps like this so widespread and persistent? If you look carefully at the following case, you can see how interpersonal blindness can crop up right before your eyes in a routine encounter.

ELLEN AND DON

Ellen, a manager in an insurance company, braced for a challenging meeting with Don, one of her subordinates. Don was bright, talented, and willing to work, just as Ellen had hoped when she hired him fresh out of college several months earlier. But his attitude was another matter. Graduating in a year when jobs were scarce, Don had accepted the administrative support role that Ellen offered him, but he wasn't happy about it. He continually complained that as a college graduate, he was underpaid and overqualified for the job. Now Ellen had an opening for an underwriter and had decided to offer Don a position as a trainee.

We'll eavesdrop on an abridged version of their conversation. Note that the right-hand column shows what they said to one another, while the left column shows what Ellen was thinking and feeling, but not saying (based on her recollections after the meeting). As you read, ask yourself how well Ellen is handling the leadership challenge she faced in this meeting. If you were in her shoes, would you do anything differently?

Ellen's Underlying Thoughts	What Ellen and Don Said
	Ellen: We're creating a new trainee position and want to offer it to you. The job will carry a salary increase, but let me tell you something about the job first.
I wonder if his education makes him feel that society owes him a living without any relationship to his abilities or productivity.	*Don:* OK. But the salary increase has to be substantial so I can improve my standard of living. I can't afford a car. I can't even afford to go out on a date.

(continued)

Ellen's Underlying Thoughts	What Ellen and Don Said
	Ellen: You'll start as a trainee working with an experienced underwriter. It's important work, because selecting the right risks is critical to our results. You'll deal directly with our agents. How you handle them affects their willingness to place their business with us.
How can he be so opinionated when he doesn't know anything about underwriting? How's he going to come across to the people he'll have to work with? The job requires judgment and willingness to listen.	*Don:* I'm highly educated. I can do anything I set my mind to. I could do the job of a supervisor right now. I don't see how risk selection is that difficult.
	Ellen: Don, we believe you're highly intelligent. You'll find you can learn many new skills working with an experienced underwriter. I'm sure many of the things you know today came from talented professors and teachers. Remember, one of the key elements in this job is your willingness to work closely with other people and to listen to their opinions.
That's the first positive response I've heard.	*Don:* I'm looking for something that will move me ahead. I'd like to move into the new job as soon as possible.
	Ellen: Our thought is to move you into this position immediately. We'll outline a training schedule for you. On-the-job and classroom learning, with testing at the end of each week.
We owe him a chance, but I doubt he'll succeed. He's got some basic problems.	*Don:* Testing is no problem. I think you'll find I score extremely high in anything I do.

At first glance, this conversation might seem routine, almost ho-hum. Look a little deeper, though, and you see how far it went off the rails. Don can't understand why no one recognizes his talents, but has no clue that his actions continually backfire. He wants to impress Ellen, but his obsessive self-promotion reinforces his image as an arrogant candidate bound for failure. Don doesn't know this, and Ellen doesn't tell him. Instead, she tells him, "We think you're intelligent," at a moment when she's feeling, "You're opinionated and don't listen." She has good reason to doubt Don's listening skills, as he doesn't seem to get the message that she's worried about his people skills. If he can't listen to his boss, what's the chance that he'll hear anyone else? Yet she leaves the meeting with the intention of moving Don into a new position while expecting that he'll fail. She colludes in a potential train wreck by skirting the topic of Don's self-defeating behavior. In protecting herself and Don from a potentially uncomfortable encounter, Ellen helps to ensure that no one learns anything.

There's nothing unusual about the encounter between Ellen and Don. Similar things happen all the time. The Dons of the world dig themselves into a hole. The Ellens help them shovel. One management expert, Chris Argyris, calls it "skilled incompetence"—using well-practiced skills to produce the opposite of what you intend.[1] Don wants Ellen to appreciate his university-acquired virtues. Instead, he strengthens her belief that he's arrogant and naive. Ellen wants Don to recognize his limitations, but unintentionally reassures him that he's fine as he is. This sort of interpersonal misfire happens to all of us—more often than we realize. We don't walk our talk. Others notice the gap, but don't tell us. We see inconsistencies in others but not in ourselves. As a result, no one learns much, and ineffectiveness reigns unchecked.

This is one major reason that leaders do strange and unproductive things at work. They say one thing and do another, oblivious to their hypocrisy. They keep making the same mistakes, but feel insulted by feedback and reject offers of help or coaching. They rehash tired clichés ("People are our most important asset"; "Work smarter, not harder"), yet can't understand why everyone ignores them.

The question of personal blindness has perplexed people since ancient times. Some twenty-five hundred years ago, Lao-tzu, a very wise Chinese philosopher, got to the heart of the issue: "Those who know others are wise. Those who know themselves are enlightened."* In the old days, the enlightened were scarce, and hypocrites were abundant. Look around your organization. You may conclude that not much has changed. In growing up, most of us have learned to build a self-image grounded in fashionable virtues. We hold on to these saintly self-images because they're a ticket to getting respect from others—and from ourselves.

But daily life often presents situations where acting on virtue is inconvenient. If we held to our espoused values, we might not keep the boss happy. Someone else might get that promotion we really want, or we might be on the losing side in a political scrap. So it's tempting to let virtue take a backseat to self-interest. It's a way to get through life's daily challenges without too much pain and suffering. But it would be awkward and uncomfortable to notice that we are inconsistent. Almost no one wants to see themselves as dishonest or devious, so why not just gloss over inconsistencies and pat ourselves on the back for being realistic and practical?

Staying blind is easier than you might think because we are all unconscious coconspirators in a social contract to keep each other comfortably unaware of discrepancies. We saw it in the conversation between Ellen and Don, and it's right before your eyes in countless business meetings. Here's the bottom line for leaders: regardless of how you see yourself, what matters is how you're seen by those you hope to lead. The question is, how do you make sure you're in touch with your constituents?

SELF-AWARENESS

Leaders develop self-awareness through ongoing learning about their actions and their impact on others. It's hard to know how others see you unless they tell you. Often, they don't. Or they do it badly. And much of the time, we're not sure we want them to. We get caught between the need to know and the fear of finding out. So we often forgo the feedback opportunities that are available. This is a major reason that so many organizations have implemented one version or another of 360-degree feedback, which they hope will give people the feedback they need but aren't sure they want, or don't know how to get on their own.

---

*Lao-tzu, quoted in T. Cleary, *The Essential Tao*. San Francisco: HarperCollins, 1992, p. 29.

Such activities are often invaluable, but they're not sufficient as a substitute for ongoing learning. Too many wannabe leaders make the mistake of believing that they should present themselves as not needing to learn from anyone because they already have all the answers. Smart leaders know better, and, if you understand a few basic principles of interpersonal feedback, you can accelerate your own learning and perhaps improve others' as well.

1. Ask and you shall receive

People often withhold feedback because they're not sure you really want it. Asking is the easiest way to get others to open up. Skill in framing the right questions helps, and persistence helps even more. If you simply ask a friend or colleague, "What did you think about my [report/speech/tie/dress]," the first response you get will often amount to vague reassurance ("Seemed fine to me."). Not much help. Follow up with more specific probes: "What do you think worked best?" "What could I have done to make it better?" "What message do you think the audience took away?" People are reluctant to tell us more than we want to know. Persistence and specificity make your requests clear and credible.

2. Say thank you

The risk of asking for feedback is that you may not like what you hear. If that's true, say so, because the other person will sense it. But be sure to thank anyone who tries to help. If you respond to a gift by rejecting it, criticizing it, or inducing guilt, the flow of future offerings will dry up fast.

3. Ask before giving

Feedback can do more harm than good. When someone doesn't want it, catching him or her off guard will usually breed suspicion and defensiveness rather than listening. How do you know if feedback is welcome? Much of the time, people aren't expecting or even thinking about it. You can usually find out with a few simple questions. One gentle but reliable approach is to ask how they felt about whatever they did: "How did you feel your presentation went?" "How do you see your role on this team?" This kind of question gets others thinking. They may ask for your reactions or, at least, give you an opening to ask them if they'd like to hear more. In any event, their response will help you assess whether they'll welcome your input.

4. When asked, give your best

With or without prompting, people will sometimes solicit your reactions to something they did. Resist the temptation to offer reassuring platitudes, but don't jump to the opposite extreme of brutal confrontation: "I can't tell if you're lazy or just stupid!" Instead, describe as specifically as you can what you saw and how you reacted. It's not much help to tell someone, for example, "The whole presentation was a flop." A more specific version of the same message might be, "Your presentation made more points than I could keep up with; after a while, I lost track of your main message."

5. Tell the truth

This is familiar advice that almost everyone endorses and almost everyone violates. The primary barrier is fear. We'd say what we think—if we weren't afraid of the consequences. Take the following conversation between a boss and a subordinate. They're both about to be killed (along with some other people whose fate is in their hands). Why? Two reasons. First, the boss has made a bad mistake, though he doesn't know it or can't admit it. Second, the subordinate is offering subtle hints instead of being direct about his concerns.

The boss is the captain of a jet airplane (in this case a DC-8 carrying cargo for the U.S. Air Force). The subordinate is his copilot. They are flying an approach into Cold Bay, Alaska. The airport is surrounded by mountains, and there are only two safe routes in. Both pilots know this, and both are looking at the same approach chart. But the captain, who is flying the plane, is off track. Looking out the window won't help, because it's dark and they're in the clouds.

(5:36 A.M.)

> *Captain:* Where's your DME? [Translation: How far are we from the airport?]
>
> *Copilot:* I don't have a reading. Last reading was forty miles.

(5:37 A.M.)

    Copilot: Are you going to make a procedure turn?

    Captain: No, I . . . I wasn't going to.

(Pause)

    Copilot: What kind of terrain are we flying over?

    Captain: Mountains everywhere.

(Pause)
(5:39 A.M.)

    Copilot: We should be a little higher, shouldn't we?

    Captain: No, forty DME [forty miles from the airport], you're all right.

(5:40 A.M.)

    Captain: I'll go up a little bit higher here. No reason to stay down that low so long.

(The captain climbs briefly to four thousand feet, then starts down again.)
(5:41 A.M.)

    Copilot: The altimeter is alive. [Translation: We're real close to those mountains.]

(5:42 A.M.)

    Copilot: Radio altimeters. Hey, John, we're off course! Four hundred feet from something!

Six seconds later, the airplane was destroyed when it crashed into a mountain.[2]

The conversation captured on the cockpit voice recorder makes it clear that the copilot was worried. But instead of saying so, he tried gentle hints ("What kind of terrain are we flying over?"). He became direct only when it was too late ("Hey, John, we're off course!").

Similar cockpit dynamics may have contributed to the crash of an Asiana Airlines Boeing 777 at San Francisco in July 2013. The captain flying the airplane was a highly experienced pilot, but he was new to the 777 and still learning. (He was transitioning from Airbus equipment with somewhat different control systems.) The captain later told investigators that he was feeling very stressed during the approach to San Francisco, though he didn't say that during the flight. He thought he had the controls set to maintain the correct speed automatically, but he was mistaken, and the plane gradually fell below its target speed. The experienced check pilot who was flying as a monitor and coach should have detected any significant deviations from correct procedures, but either he didn't notice or was too polite to say anything. Airspeed is a critical factor in landing an airplane, and an airspeed indicator was plainly visible. Although it is conceivable that neither of these two experienced pilots realized they were getting into trouble, it is more likely that at least one of them did know but chose not to mention it, perhaps for fear of making a bad situation worse. About a minute before the accident, a junior relief pilot sitting in the jump seat politely commented, "Sink rate, sir" (a gentle hint that the plane was descending too quickly). He repeated the remark five seconds later, but no one seemed to get the message. The captain and check pilot continued on a path to catastrophe, making routine callouts. The plane approached the runway too low and too slow, but only at eight seconds before the crash did the check pilot twice say "speed." Less than two seconds before impact, he called, "Oh [expletive], go around." That order to abort the landing came too late.[3] The plane stalled, the rear end hit a seawall at the end of the runway, and the tail separated. Three teenage girls in the back of the plane were killed, and about 180 other passengers were injured, some critically.

Most situations you encounter at work aren't likely to be matters of life and death. But the costs of not speaking up can still be very serious. It's tempting to muddle along and avoid rocking the boat. If you're in a truly toxic workplace, that may be a safe and sane option, even if it mires you deeper in a rut. But you'll become a better leader if you learn from others and they learn from you. It's a rare and potent skill.

LEADERSHIP SKILLS: ADVOCACY AND INQUIRY

It's easy to see that leaders need to communicate clearly and persuasively to advocate effectively on behalf of their mission and constituents. But many leaders fail to recognize that they also need to be good at inquiry. Probing with questions and observation enables them to learn from experience and to acquire information they need if they are to understand what's going on. Leaders are high on advocacy when they are communicating clearly and effectively. They are high on inquiry when they are actively asking questions and encouraging feedback to get important information (see Figure 5.1).

Leaders need continuing practice and feedback to enhance their skills in both advocacy and inquiry. The ability to combine them leads to a much better chance of being effective in the challenging environment of an airline cockpit, or the more mundane circumstances of Ellen's encounter with Don. Let's revisit their dialogue to examine how Ellen might have been more direct so as to generate learning for Don—and maybe for herself as well. Assume that the conversation starts exactly as before, but Ellen responds differently to Don because she follows two simple rules: (1) she says what's on her mind, and (2) she asks questions in order to learn—and to confront.

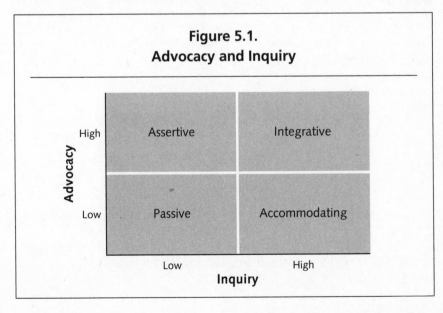

Figure 5.1.
Advocacy and Inquiry

High	Assertive	Integrative
Low	Passive	Accommodating
	Low	High

Advocacy (vertical axis)

Inquiry (horizontal axis)

Ellen's Underlying Thoughts	What Ellen and Don Said
	Ellen: We're creating a new trainee position and want to offer it to you. The job will carry a salary increase, but let me tell you something about the job first.
I wonder if his education makes him feel that society owes him a living without any relationship to his abilities or productivity.	*Don:* OK. But the salary increase has to be substantial so I can improve my standard of living. I can't afford a car. I can't even afford to go out on a date.
	Ellen: I understand you want to earn more, but are you aware that pay is based on how much you contribute rather than how much you want?
	Don: Um, I guess.
	Ellen: You'll start as a trainee working with an experienced underwriter. It's important work, because selecting the right risks is critical to our results. You'll deal directly with our agents. How you handle them affects their willingness to place their business with us.
How can he be so opinionated when he doesn't know anything about underwriting? How's he going to come across to the people he'll have to work with? The job requires judgment and willingness to listen.	*Don:* I'm highly educated. I can do anything I set my mind to. I could do the job of a supervisor right now. I don't see how risk selection is that difficult.
	Ellen: Have you ever been a supervisor or an underwriter?
	Don: Well, not exactly, but I still don't see that they're that hard.
	Ellen: When you tell me you already know how to do something you've never done, can you see why I worry that you're being unrealistic about yourself?

Ellen's Underlying Thoughts	What Ellen and Don Said

Don: I still say I can do whatever I put my mind to.

Ellen: Right now, can you put your mind to listening to what I'm saying?

Don: (pauses, looking surprised) Uh, well, yeah, that's what I'm doing.

Ellen: Good. I want to be sure you understand that we expect a trainee to start with the attitude, "I'm here to learn," not "I already know everything." Are you comfortable with that?

That's the first positive response I've heard.

Don: Well, OK, if that's what I need to do.

Ellen: Don, we believe you're highly intelligent. You'll find you can learn many new skills working with an experienced underwriter. I'm sure many of the things you know today came from talented professors and teachers. Remember, one of the key elements in this job is your willingness to work closely with other people and to listen to their opinions.

Don: I'm looking for something that will move me ahead. I'd like to move into the new job as soon as possible.

Ellen: Our thought is to move you into this position immediately. We'll outline a training schedule for you. On-the-job and classroom learning, with testing at the end of each week.

Don: Testing is no problem. I think you'll find I score extremely high in anything I do.

Ellen: Does that include listening and openness to learning?

Don: Um, sure.

In this conversation, unlike the one at the beginning of the chapter, Ellen spoke directly to the issues that concerned her, and deftly punctured Don's bravado with a series of questions designed to trigger reflection on his part. Instead of letting Don off the hook with his inflated claims, she asked him to explain and gently confronted him. When, for example, he insisted that he scores high on anything he does, she asked if that included listening to her. Don was surprised by a question that nudged him to think about a skill he'd neglected. Ellen combined advocacy with inquiry in her statement, "I want to be sure you understand that we expect a trainee to start with the attitude, 'I'm here to learn,' not 'I already know everything.' Are you comfortable with that?" She clarifies expectations, and her question at the end is powerful because it asks for acknowledgment and commitment.

Ellen, if she is wise, will not expect Don to be transformed by one conversation. But in questioning rather than ignoring Don's self-aggrandizement, she prods Don to reflect on his actions and to realize that some of his patterns are self-defeating. It's hard to make someone learn, but you improve the odds when you interrupt ineffective patterns and provoke self-reflection. Good leaders are adept at both advocacy and inquiry.

CONCLUSION

Leaders spend most of their time communicating with others, but if they don't know how others see them, they are flying blind, and their messages will often go awry. It is hard to become a great leader without being a great listener and learner. Interpersonal communication is central to leadership, but it is inherently rife with traps and snares that leave both leaders and subordinates confused and frustrated. Leaders contribute to this muddled interplay through their own personal blindness and their lack of awareness of basic principles and skills, such as advocacy and inquiry, that improve leaders' ability to communicate with others more effectively.

We've looked at the power of the structural and human resource frames. Both are essential to enlightened leadership, but even together, they are still not enough. Neither grapples very well with the political dynamics that are an inevitable feature of social life. That's where we'll go in Chapter Six, the first of the political chapters.

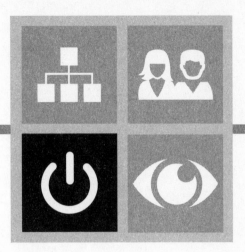

PART 4

Political Leadership

Political leaders see a world of contests among individuals and interest groups competing over scarce resources. They recognize that they need to plunge into the political arena to move their organization where it needs to go.

- Political leaders clarify what they want and what they can get.
- They assess the distribution of power and interests.
- They build linkages to key stakeholders.
- They persuade first, negotiate second, and coerce only if necessary.

The Leader as Politician

In the 2014 Tournament of Roses Parade in Pasadena, California, bitter controversy surfaced around a float featuring two men joining in a lavish same-sex wedding ceremony. It was a first for the parade, welcome to some and anathema to others. It was only one of many skirmishes in a conflict that had been swirling around the United States for years. The battle lines divided political parties, neighborhoods, towns, church congregations, families, and legislatures, among many other groups. The U.S. Supreme Court had struck down the federal Defense of Marriage Act, and an increasing number of states had legalized same-sex marriage, but the conflict continued and resolution seemed remote.

Same-sex marriage, of course, is only one of many contentious issues that pervade life in any nation or society. You have probably realized, perhaps painfully, that politics is an everyday feature of life. Maybe you wish it were otherwise and wonder why we can't just push politics aside and focus on getting the job done. But, like it or not, politics is here to stay. Ignoring that reality sets you up for chronic frustration and failure. We often blame politics on various individual flaws like selfishness, myopia, incompetence, and hunger for power, but the real wellsprings lie deeper—in our circumstances rather than ourselves.

Every group and organization is political, for two reasons: (1) individuals and groups have divergent interests and values, and (2) they live in a world of scarce resources. It is impossible for everybody to get everything they want. Examples are endless. Did you get the promotion you expected, or did someone else? Will a new automobile assembly plant be built in Alabama or South Carolina? Should taxpayers spring for tens of millions to build a new arena so that the local major league team won't decamp? Such conflicts inevitably spawn political maneuvering. You may not like the idea of thinking politically; many people don't because they see politics as sordid and amoral. But, like it or not, to be an effective leader, you need to understand and leverage political dynamics rather than shy away from them.

Take a look at what was at stake politically for Anne Mulcahy, who became president of Xerox in August 2001. Politically, it looked as though the deck was stacked against her. Few observers gave her much chance of success: "Xerox had $17.1 billion in debt and $154 million in cash. It was about to begin seven straight quarters of losses. The credit markets had slammed shut. An SEC investigation of the Mexico unit was about to spread to other parts of the company. Reorganizations of the sales force and the billing centers had led to chaos. In 2000 the stock fell from $63.69 a share to $4.43, the company lost 90% of its market cap, and the best and brightest headed for the exits. The board had one last chance—and, boy, was she a long shot."[1]

Warren Buffett summarized her plight succinctly: "You didn't get promoted. You went to war."[2] Yet three years later, *Businessweek* put Mulcahy on its list of the best managers of 2004. The stock was up, the company was profitable again, and Mulcahy had met earnings targets ten quarters in a row. Her success formula combined passion, hard work, and deft handling of the political challenges she faced.

Her predecessor, an import from IBM, had been fired after only thirteen months on the job, partly as a result of "executive-suite discord so intractable as to amount to corporate civil war."[3] Mulcahy understood what many would-be leaders never fully appreciate: position power is important, but it is never sufficient. Organizations and societies are networks as well as hierarchies, and the power of relationships is a crucial complement to the power of position. In simplest terms, network power amounts to the power of your friends minus the power of your enemies. Mulcahy saw and acted on the need to rally friends while converting skeptics and enemies into allies. Her deft combination of patience, persistence, and diplomacy offers an instructive example of the leader as positive politician.

POLITICAL SKILLS

The leader as politician needs to master at least four key skills: agenda setting,[4] mapping the political terrain,[5] networking and forming coalitions,[6] and bargaining and negotiating.[7] We use Mulcahy's leadership at Xerox to illuminate each of these.

Setting Agendas

Structurally, an agenda outlines a goal and a schedule of activities. Politically, it is a statement of interests and a scenario for getting the goods. In reflecting on his experience as a university president, Warren Bennis arrived at a deceptively simple observation: "It struck me that I was most effective when I knew what I wanted."[8] Whether you're a middle manager or the CEO, the first step in effective political leadership is creating an agenda with two major elements: a vision balancing the long-term interests of key parties, and a strategy for achieving the vision that recognizes competing internal and external forces.

There is an intimate tie between developing a vision and gathering information. You need to understand how key constituents think and what they care about to ensure that your agenda meshes with their concerns. In the course of gathering information, you can also plant seeds, "leaving the kernel of an idea behind and letting it germinate and blossom so that it begins to float around the system from many sources other than the innovator."[9]

Mulcahy's vision had two prongs: an immediate goal of staving off bankruptcy, and a long-term vision of making Xerox once again a great company. But vision is merely an illusion unless you have a strategy that recognizes major forces working for and against your agenda. Mulcahy saw that her most pressing task was to build confidence and support among internal and external constituents who could make or break her effort to put the company back on its feet.

Mapping the Political Terrain

It is foolhardy to plunge into a minefield without knowing where the explosives are buried and that a safe path exists. Yet managers unwittingly push ahead all the time. They launch a new initiative with little or no effort to scout and chart the political turf. A simple way to develop a political map for any situation is to create a two-dimensional diagram showing players (who is in the game), power (how much clout each player is likely to wield), and interests (what each player wants). Figure 6.1 illustrates the political map that Mulcahy faced on her first day in the job. Her strongest allies are Xerox insiders, who may not all be reliable, and their clout is relatively low. Some of the most talented players at Xerox have been leaving for other jobs because they have doubts about the future, and they're tired of internal discord. Customers are free agents—they could stick with Xerox, or abandon what may become a sinking ship. The board is a powerful player wanting her to succeed, but it also has fiduciary responsibility for the enterprise's financial health. Her biggest challenge is the bankers and financial advisers. The bankers are in a dilemma. They don't want Xerox to go bankrupt because their loans might not be paid back. But it would be worse to throw good money after bad, and Xerox's weak cash position means that it can't survive without a credit lifeline. Mulcahy needs the advisers to help her find a path through the financial wilderness, but they insist that bankruptcy is the only option.

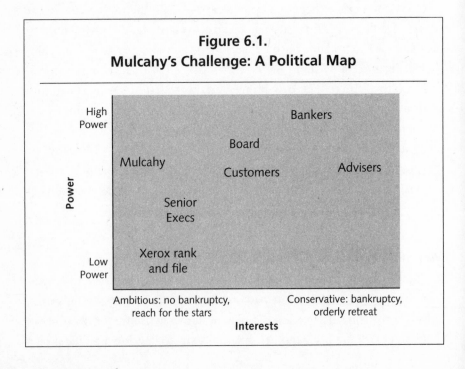

Figure 6.1.
Mulcahy's Challenge: A Political Map

The map makes it clear that Mulcahy will fail unless she can get key external constituents to move in her direction. The map in Figure 6.1 is a starting point and a guide to key questions: How well does she know the political landscape? Has she identified the key players? How do they line up on the issues? Does she have the power she needs? If not, how can she get it?

Misreading the political landscape can lead to costly errors. There's a good chance you've never heard of John LeBoutillier. That's because he made one mistake that undermined a promising political career. Shortly after he was elected to Congress from a wealthy district in Long Island, LeBoutillier fired up his audience at the New York Republican convention with the colorful quip that Speaker of the House Thomas P. O'Neill was "fat, bloated and out of control, just like the Federal budget." Asked to comment, the usually voluble O'Neill was terse: "I wouldn't know the man from a cord of wood."[10] Two years later, LeBoutillier unexpectedly lost his bid for reelection to an unknown opponent who didn't have the money to mount a serious campaign—until a mysterious flood of contributions poured in from all over America. When LeBoutillier later ran into O'Neill, he admitted sheepishly, "I guess you were more popular than I thought you were."[11] LeBoutillier learned the hard way that misreading the political map and overlooking the power of potential players can lead to catastrophe. That's why it's critical to treat the map as a work in progress—a guide to be tested as you move along.

If you put yourself in Anne Mulcahy's position, would you have taken the job, knowing how big the problems were? And if you had accepted, how would you have tackled the challenges ahead?

Networking and Building Coalitions

With an agenda and a map in hand, Mulcahy can move to developing relationships with key constituents. The top job gives Mulcahy substantial authority, but also makes her dependent on the cooperation of a large number of internal and external players. The first task in building networks and coalitions is to figure out whose help you need. The second is to develop relationships so that people will be there when you need them. The political map helps pinpoint the key constituents. The next question is how to get their support. In her study of successful internal change agents, Rosabeth

Kanter found that they typically started by getting their boss on board, and then moved to "preselling," or "making cheerleaders": "peers, managers of related functions, stakeholders in the issue, potential collaborators, and sometimes even customers would be approached individually, in one-on-one meetings that gave people a chance to influence the project and [gave] the innovator the maximum opportunity to sell it. Seeing them alone and on their territory was important: the rule was to act as if each person were *the* most important one for the project's success."[12]

If you're Mulcahy and take that advice seriously, you'd be doing a lot of travel—and that's what she did: "Constantly on the move, Mulcahy met with bankers, reassured customers, galvanized employees. She sometimes visited three cities a day."[13] She promised to go anywhere to save a Xerox customer. She also located key allies who could provide skills or information she needed. She had no finance background and asked a financial analyst she had worked with previously to teach her Balance Sheet 101. She found another ally in Ursula Burns, who was planning to bail out of Xerox before Mulcahy recruited her. Burns became Mulcahy's deputy and enforcer who managed internal issues while Mulcahy focused more on the outside. Senior executives soon learned that it was better to meet their targets than to have to explain to Burns why they had missed.

Once you cultivate allies, you can move to "horse trading": promising rewards in exchange for resources and support. Mulcahy met constantly with bankers and financial advisers; she gradually, painstakingly convinced them that she and Xerox had a future in which they could afford to invest. Internally, she needed a strong and loyal executive team. She met personally with more than one hundred top executives to sell them on the opportunities and ask them directly if they were willing to be "all about Xerox."

The basic point is simple: leaders need friends and allies to get things done. To sew up support, they need to build coalitions. Rationalists and romantics sometimes react with horror to this scenario. Why should you have to play political games to get something accepted if it's the right thing to do? One of the classics of French drama, Molière's *The Misanthrope*, tells the story of a protagonist whose rigid rejection of all things political is destructive for him and everyone involved. The point that Molière made four centuries ago still holds: it is hard to dislike politics without also disliking people. Like it or not, political dynamics are inevitable under three conditions most managers face every day: ambiguity, diversity, and scarcity.

Bargaining and Negotiation

We often associate bargaining with commercial, legal, and labor relations transactions. From a political perspective, bargaining is central to decision making. Negotiation makes a difference whenever two or more parties with some interests in common and others in conflict need to reach agreement. Labor and management may agree that a firm should make money and offer good jobs to employees, but part ways on how to balance pay and profitability. A fundamental challenge in negotiations is balancing win-win and win-lose. Advocates of win-win believe that better results come when parties are creative and cooperative in searching for mutually beneficial solutions. The win-lose view depicts bargaining as a hard, tough process in which you do what it takes to get as much as you can.

Fisher and Ury developed one of the best-known win-win approaches to negotiation in their classic *Getting to Yes*. In their view, people too often engage in "positional bargaining." They stake out positions and then reluctantly make concessions to reach agreement. To Fisher and Ury, positional bargaining is inefficient and misses opportunities to create something that's better for everyone. They propose an alternative: "principled bargaining," built around four strategies.[14]

The first strategy separates people from the problem. The stress and tension of negotiations can easily escalate into anger and personal attack. The result is that a negotiator sometimes wants to defeat or hurt the other party at almost any cost. Because every negotiation involves both substance and relationship, the wise negotiator will "deal with the people as human beings and with the problem on its merits."[15]

Fisher and Ury's second strategy focuses on interests, not positions. Being locked into a particular position, you might overlook better ways to achieve your goal. A famous example is the 1978 Camp David Accords between Israel and Egypt. The sides were at an impasse over where to draw the boundary between the two countries. Israel wanted to keep part of the Sinai; Egypt wanted all of it back. Resolution became possible only when they looked at underlying interests. Israel was concerned about security:

no Egyptian tanks on the border. Egypt was concerned about sovereignty: the Sinai had been part of Egypt from the time of the pharaohs. The parties agreed on a plan that gave all of the Sinai back to Egypt while demilitarizing large parts of it. That solution led to a durable peace agreement.

Fisher and Ury's third strategy is to invent options for mutual gain instead of locking on to the first alternative that comes to mind. Having more options increases the chance of a better outcome. Mulcahy's financial advisers insisted that Xerox's cash position was hopeless and that she had to declare bankruptcy. Mulcahy looked for other options—and found them. Some were painful, but, she concluded, necessary. One of her worst moments was closing down a division that she had built, releasing people whom she had hired. It wasn't their fault, she said, and the only thing she could do was walk the halls and say, "I'm sorry."[16]

Fisher and Ury's fourth strategy is to insist on objective criteria—standards of fairness for both substance and procedure. Agreeing on criteria at the beginning of negotiations can produce optimism and momentum, while reducing the use of devious or provocative tactics. When a school board and a teachers' union are at loggerheads over the size of a pay increase, they can look for independent standards, such as the rate of inflation or the terms of settlement in other districts. A classic example of fair procedure finds two sisters deadlocked over how to divide the last wedge of pie between them. They agree that one will cut the pie into two pieces and the other will choose the piece that she wants.

How does a leader decide how to balance win-win and win-lose approaches to bargaining? At least two questions are important: How much opportunity is there for a win-win solution? and Will I have to work with these people again? If an agreement can make everyone better off, creating value is the right course. If you expect to work with the same people in the future, it is risky to use scorched-earth tactics that leave anger and mistrust in their wake. Leaders who get a reputation for being manipulative, self-interested, or untrustworthy have a hard time building the networks and coalitions they need for future success.

Mulcahy was primarily a win-win bargainer. She invested heavily in meetings with bankers to assure them that Xerox really would pay back its $7 billion credit line. It was a tough sell, but bankers saw the win-win. There was one issue on which she was a stubborn positional bargainer. Whenever anyone tried to tell her that Xerox would be better off in Chapter 11, her response was firm: "Bankruptcy's never a win. I'm not going there until there's no other decision to be made."[17]

Mulcahy's passion, persistence, and patience eventually paid off. She cut expenses to a manageable level and got the bankers to provide the cash Xerox needed while she rebuilt a leaner, more effective business. She had to make some painful decisions, but Xerox emerged from the crisis as a profitable and growing enterprise.

A CASE EXAMPLE: THE TROUBLED AUDITOR

Suppose that you're working as the vice president of internal audit at the only big employer in your town, the headquarters of a major national corporation. It has not been easy, but over time you've earned credibility with your skeptical CEO by showing that your unit can cut waste and improve the bottom line. Life has been good—until the day a worried executive tells you that corporate accounting has taken a cool $400 million out of a reserve account and used it to improve the company's bottom line. Only months have passed since bad accounting killed Enron, so this is a red flag. You ask an Arthur Andersen auditor to explain the transaction, but he brushes you off. Then you bring up the issue at a meeting of the corporate audit committee, and your boss, the chief financial officer, gets so angry you begin to wonder if your job is safe.

You're the family breadwinner, and your spouse is home with your children. Your company is the only game in town, so if you lose this job, your fallback might be working the counter at a fast-food restaurant. This transaction doesn't pass the smell test, but it's a dangerous hot potato that your boss has told you to drop. In those circumstances, would you drop it or pursue it? If you decide to pursue, how would you go about it? What's your agenda? What does the political map look like? Whom do you need as allies? What's your negotiating stance?

This story may sound like something out of a John Grisham novel, but it's very real. The troubled auditor was Cynthia Cooper, vice president of internal audit at WorldCom.[18] She was a smart and dogged professional whose mother had taught her not to let people intimidate her. She decided she had to look further. Her agenda was straightforward: keep digging until she got the truth. She knew that the political map was unfavorable. Her boss, the CFO, and his boss, the CEO, would block her investigation. She was in the classic position of a guerrilla leader: a frontal assault was suicide, and stealth was her best option. In effect, she took her bosses off the political map by keeping them in the dark; they couldn't play in a game that they didn't know was going on. She was fortunate that one of her allies, Gene Morse, had the right permissions to get the data they needed. Morse was eager to sign on; he had moved over to Cooper's unit after a previous boss threatened to throw him out if he shared certain numbers with the auditors. Working in a windowless room, often at night after most people had gone home, Morse downloaded reams of numbers onto CD-ROMs to make sure WorldCom officials couldn't make the data disappear.

The deeper Cooper and her allies dug, the worse it got. By the beginning of June 2002, they had discovered a stunning $3 billion in questionable items. Armed with the data she needed, Cooper was now in the driver's seat on a very different political field. She confronted WorldCom's controller, who admitted the entries could not be justified. The CFO, Scott Sullivan, tried to persuade her to hold off, but she refused. On June 20, Cooper and her team shared their findings with the board of directors' audit commit-tee. The board asked Sullivan to explain, and fired him when he couldn't. On June 25, WorldCom announced that it had overstated its profits for the previous five quarters by almost $4 billion. A month later, WorldCom declared bankruptcy—at the time, the largest collapse in American corpo-rate history.

The success of Cooper and her allies in overcoming opposition to expose corporate fraud demonstrates the power of political thinking, even in uphill battles. It is unrealistic to hope that reason and data, as important as they are, will always be enough to carry the day. Mapping the politi-cal field, networking, and building alliances can turn a weak hand into a winner.

CONCLUSION

The question is not whether organizations are political but rather what kind of politics they will encompass. Political dynamics can be sordid and destructive, conspiracies crafted in smoke-filled rooms. But politics can also be a vehicle for achieving noble purposes in public forums. The political frame provides the essential tools that leaders need to understand and cope with the political dynamics they will inevitably face. Organizational change and effectiveness depend on political skills and savvy. Constructive politicians know how to fashion an agenda, map the political terrain, create a network of support, and negotiate with both allies and adversaries.

Conflict plays a key role in political dealings. This makes it very difficult for leaders who prefer calm waters to stormy seas. Unfortunately, conflict is an integral part of life in organizations. Harry Truman's terse message to leaders was, "If you can't stand the heat, stay out of the kitchen." Chapter Seven explores the roles of leaders in dealing with discord.

The Leader as Warrior and Peacemaker

Conflict is an unwelcome but inevitable feature in relationships, groups, and organizations. When it surfaces, people typically try to smooth it over or avoid it. Left untended, it intensifies and festers, undermining communication, encouraging plots and sabotage, and producing disruptive explosions. People dislike and avoid conflict because they see it as dangerous, fear the emotional turmoil it generates, or distrust their own skills in confronting it. But conflict plays an integral role in leadership, and savvy leaders recognize its benefits: "a tranquil, harmonious organization may very well be an apathetic, uncreative, stagnant, inflexible and unresponsive organization."[1] When leaders handle conflict well, they can break through logjams, stimulate innovation and learning, and make their institution a livelier and more effective place.

In this chapter, we will look at two stances that leaders can adopt in handling conflict: warrior and peacemaker. We'll examine a dramatic example of the two stances at work, with Apple's Steve Jobs epitomizing the warrior, and Walt Disney's Bob Iger serving as peacemaker. We discuss when and how leaders can adopt each role.

STEVE JOBS: THE WARRIOR

Artist, entrepreneur, futuristic visionary, and brilliant marketer—Steve Jobs was all of these. He was also an aggressive pugilist ready to slug it out for any project or cause he championed. His combat style relied more on persistence and brute force than compromise and subtlety. A case in point was his battle with Michael Eisner, the Walt Disney Studios CEO, over kids' movies. The skirmish traced back to 1986, when Jobs bought 70 percent of the computer division of Lucasfilm because he thought its technology was "really cool." Over the next several years, Jobs poured more than $50 million into the business, even as it kept losing money. As things started to turn around, he persuaded a player with deep pockets—Walt Disney Studios—to finance the studio's first feature film, *Toy Story*.[2]

The Disney deal saved the business—now called Pixar—but at a price. Disney got full ownership of the first three films, leaving Pixar with only a sliver of the revenues. After *Toy Story*'s success, Jobs flew to Hollywood and doggedly renegotiated the deal with Disney's new chief, Michael Eisner. Jobs got what he wanted: cobranding and 50 percent ownership of the next two films. But in sealing the transaction, he and Eisner got off to a bad start, initiating a rocky relationship that was to deteriorate even more as time passed. A full-scale feud emerged several years later in 2002, when Eisner publicly criticized "computer companies" for promoting digital piracy. Eisner didn't name names, but everyone knew he was talking about Apple and iTunes. Whether he wanted a war or not, he had inflamed a dangerous adversary. He and Jobs traded salvos as the Disney-Pixar deal was coming up for renewal. At that point, Eisner made one of the most common political mistakes in business and life: he misread the balance of power and escalated a battle he was destined to lose.

Jobs, as a shrewd warrior, began to assemble his allies. He cultivated relationships with key members of Disney's board, including Walt's nephew, Roy Disney. Jobs spread the word that there would be no new deal as long as Eisner was CEO. Eisner countered with a memo to the board insisting that Disney was in the driver's seat because it owned all of Pixar's characters—Woody, Buzz Lightyear, and the whole gang. In addition, he maintained that Pixar's bargaining position was about to get weaker because he'd seen their next film and it wasn't very good. The memo back-fired. Someone leaked it to the *Los Angeles Times*, and Jobs was predictably infuriated. Even worse, Eisner had seriously underestimated Pixar's next film. *Finding Nemo* won the Oscar for animated films and became Disney's most successful film yet.

Two proud and stubborn warriors dug in for a battle that many observers viewed as more about ego than substance. Eisner forced Roy Disney off the board and threatened to make *Toy Story III* with no help from Pixar. Jobs countered that he was cutting off negotiations with Disney and broadcast his assessment that, except for Pixar, Disney had produced nothing but flops in recent years. The impasse was broken only when the Disney board decided they needed Pixar more than they needed Eisner. They fired their CEO and replaced him with his deft, good-humored second-in-command, Bob Iger, "even though Eisner reportedly told directors Iger wasn't up to the top job."[3]

ENTER BOB IGER: THE PEACEMAKER

Bob Iger began his career as a weatherman on a local television station in upstate New York. He later joined ABC and worked his way up to become president of ABC Television. When Disney acquired Capital Cities/ABC, Iger came over to serve as chief operating officer under Eisner. Described as a leader who does more listening than talking, Iger "was as sensible and solid as those around him were volatile" and "had a disciplined calm, which helped him deal with large egos."[4] His friend Warren Buffett offered a similar impression: "He's always calm and rational and makes sense. He runs things without a heavy hand."[5] In viewing the Eisner-Jobs conflagration, Iger observed, "Every negotiation needs to be resolved by compromises. Neither one of them is a master of compromise."[6] As soon as he became CEO, Iger embarked on peacemaking initiatives. He reconciled with Roy Disney and brought him back into the fold. He worked even harder to repair the relationship with Jobs and Pixar.

Iger agreed with Jobs on the issue that mattered most: Disney's animated hits in the previous decade had all come from Pixar. It helped that Iger and Jobs had worked together previously on a deal to put some of ABC's shows on the iPod. Iger had come on stage at one of Jobs's signature product launches to celebrate the partnership. Iger recalled, "It signaled my way of operating, which was 'Make love not war.' We had been at war with Roy Disney, Comcast, Apple, and Pixar. I wanted to fix all that, Pixar most of all."[7] As soon as he replaced Eisner, Iger got on the phone to tell

Jobs he wanted to make a deal. It took extended negotiations. Even though Eisner made a last-ditch effort to throw a monkey wrench into the works, Disney agreed to buy Pixar for $7.1 billion in stock. Jobs became a billionaire and Disney's biggest shareholder, and Pixar's leadership took over Disney's animation.

ORCHESTRATING CONFLICT: RAISE OR LOWER THE FLAME?

Bob Iger and Steve Jobs embody two basic approaches to conflict: those of the peacemaker and the warrior. Organizations need both. Warriors are resolute fighters who raise the heat and intensify the conflict. Peacemakers work to lower the temperature and defuse conflict in the hope of minimizing destructive, lose-lose dynamics. Blessed are the peacemakers, but great leaders are often warriors. You will be a more versatile and powerful leader if you know how and when to play either role.

The Peacemaker: Cooling the Flame

The battle between Michael Eisner and Steve Jobs typifies conflict situations that carry the potential for mutual destruction. Conflict takes on personal and emotional overtones, and the parties feel convinced that "we're right and they're wrong." Such highly charged situations touch hot buttons for leaders and create the risk that raw emotions and jangled nerves will impair their capacity to produce a positive outcome. Like Bob Iger, a leader may be caught somewhere between contending parties, hoping to find some mutually acceptable resolution. But finding a suitable middle path is rarely easy. It requires adaptation by parties wed to their current stance. Leadership often has to challenge existing beliefs and emotional investments, asking others to review where they stand and what they know or value.

This is not easy, but leadership experts Ronald Heifetz and Martin Linsky offer an optimistic note: "The hope of leadership lies in the capacity to deliver disturbing news and raise difficult questions in a way that people can absorb, prodding them to take up the message rather than ignore it or kill the messenger."[8] They emphasize the importance of distinguishing technical from adaptive problems. A technical problem is one for which available information and procedures can produce a solution that meets accepted criteria for success. When leaders have the information and expertise to make a workable decision, they can do what their constituents expect: solve problems so everyone can move on. Adaptive problems, however, are messier. They don't offer well-defined paths to solution, and differences in values, purposes, or beliefs make it hard to agree about what constitutes a good option. Unilateral decisions usually fail because the audience isn't ready. Adaptive leaders help parties understand why the problem is so difficult and become more willing to find and accept a solution.

Several guidelines can help peacemakers do their work well.

Be Patient

When the baby is not yet ready to be born, rushing the process makes things worse. Skilled peacemakers understand that conflict resolution takes time, effort, and learning. This often requires working against the grain and being prepared for predictable resistance and criticism. Rather than fulfilling others' expectations for quick answers, leaders need to pose questions and encourage dialogue.

Listen and Inquire: Understand Parties' Interests, Thinking, and Feelings

Inquiry and listening are critical for two reasons. One is to ensure that you understand the political map: Who are the players? What are their interests? What moves are they likely to make? Answers to these questions help you anticipate the flow of the game and assess which solutions are feasible and which are not. Listening is also critical because parties who feel they have been heard and understood are better able to put emotions aside and focus on solving the problem.

Engage the Parties: Put People to Work

Consider the case of John Alden, the academic vice president in a large state university. Under a mandate to make significant budget cuts, he invited his deans to participate in the process, but they persuaded him to make the decisions himself. After all, they told him, he had the broader institutional perspective needed for something so important. Alden collected data, developed criteria, and conducted a thoughtful analysis to generate a list of tentative cuts. He intended them as a starting point for discussion, but when they became public, *he* became the problem. It was "Alden's plan" and "the vice president's budget axe." Those who liked his proposals mostly watched from the sidelines. The opponents were vocal, visible, and persistent. The ensuing firestorm marked the end of a promising leadership career. For Alden, it was painful and devastating, and he chose to leave the academy to work in the private sector. Meanwhile, the campus could blame him and evade responsibility for addressing the financial realities.

When parties are deeply in conflict, leaders need to orchestrate a process that engages them in understanding the issues and searching for a way forward. The leadership task is to bring together different sides to engage in a conversation that the parties would often prefer to avoid. Leaders need to create arenas with rules, roles, and referees and be prepared to tightly manage the exchange. When these tasks are done well, they increase the chances that participants can learn from the dialogue and find a way out of the impasse. Alden intended to move in that direction, but backed off in response to the deans' successful effort at upward delegation.

Defuse Emotion and Depersonalize Criticism

Conflict stirs up powerful feelings. The challenge for leaders is to recognize and acknowledge those emotions without being overwhelmed by them. Others' feelings may seem unreasonable or wrong, but that does not make them any less real. You can listen and acknowledge without agreeing, and that often helps lower the heat.

It is inevitable that leaders will make mistakes and enemies. Even when leaders are right, some people will think they're wrong or will react emotionally to what they experience. A conflict situation is the wrong place for a leader to look for love. When criticism wounds and feels unfair, remember that others are usually responding more to your role in a messy situation than to you personally. One of the hardest and most important tests of professionalism is to "keep your head when all about you are losing theirs and blaming it on you."[9] When your emotions run hot, as they sometimes will, slow down, take a deep breath, and buy time before doing anything rash. "Go to the balcony" and try to gain another perspective on the action. Talk it over with someone you can trust. Stay on task, and focus on the purposes you're trying to achieve. That makes it easier to depersonalize an emotionally charged situation and to keep your emotions from goading you into impetuous and regrettable actions.

The Warrior: Turning Up the Heat

When conflict burns too hot, it overwhelms reason, undermines dialogue, and increases the likelihood of destructive warfare. Such cases call for peacemakers. But, in business and elsewhere, you often face competitors or opponents whose goals and values are fundamentally incompatible with your own. If you win, they lose, and vice versa.

The combativeness we saw in Steve Jobs is not exceptional among the entrepreneurs who have built great business enterprises. It's true of contemporary leaders such as Microsoft founder Bill Gates and Oracle's notoriously feisty Larry Ellison. It was also true a century ago. Kodak founder George Eastman was a warrior as well as an innovator. "Peace extends only to private life," he observed. "In business it is war all the time."[10] Cornelius Vanderbilt on occasion defended his business interests with his fists. In his later years, he was less physical but no less combative. On one famous occasion, some associates tried to wrest control of his company while he was away on business. He fired off a famous letter:

> Gentlemen:
> You have undertaken to cheat me. I won't sue you, for the law
> is too slow. I'll ruin you.
> Yours truly,
> Cornelius Vanderbilt.[11]

Ruin them he did.

These examples all tell the same story: leaders often need to confront conflict head-on rather than fear it and back away. Both modern research on leadership and ancient wisdom on strategy teach that successful warriors combine four basic ingredients: spirit, mind, skill, and power.[12] *Spirit* gives warriors passion, courage, and persistence, the "fire in the belly" that propels them forward in the face of the perennial challenges of combat: risk, confusion, danger, obstacles, and reversals. *Mind* gives warriors the direction and guidance that enables them to recognize and choose the best available moves on the chessboard of life, while avoiding snares, ambushes, and blind alleys. *Skill* determines how well a leader fights and leads. *Power* furnishes the resources that enable leaders to win.

Each of these ingredients provides the warrior leader a potential path to victory: (1) overcoming a less determined or more fearful opponent with superior courage and passion; (2) outsmarting a more confused or less disciplined opponent with a better game plan or tactical superiority; (3) besting an opponent through greater skill; or (4) winning by putting stronger assets on the field—a larger force, better players, or superior weaponry.

Four guidelines can help leaders achieve victory in combat.

Fight with Passion and Persistence—or Avoid Combat

Passion, or heart, is vital to leadership. It is rooted in a deep, sometimes obsessive, personal and emotional commitment to a cause, group, or task. It is a basic quality of all great warriors and leaders. It energizes, sustains courage, and fuels persistence. It is also contagious. The leader's passion, or lack of it, is known and felt by followers. Almost anyone who worked for Steve Jobs acknowledged that he was a notoriously difficult boss, but his passion and commitment to a larger cause made it all worthwhile. Wal-Mart founder Sam Walton was all of twenty-seven years old when he started his business with the second-best variety store in tiny Newport, Arkansas, but he was always a happy warrior who loved people, and loved winning even more. His passion led him to work harder, travel more, and spend as much time as he could in his competitors' stores looking for any idea he could steal.[13]

Out-Think Opponents—Win with a Better Game Plan

Passion fuels the warrior, but without direction and discipline, passion may lead to ruin. Mind without spirit is sterile, but spirit without mind is reckless, often suicidal. The effective leader needs both. Operating in better light than your opponent gives you a substantial edge. If you know the playing field better than your opponents and know more about them than they do about you, the odds shift in your favor, even if they have superior resources.

Clear thinking is never more important than before you embark on a campaign. It is foolish to go into combat without knowing what you are fighting for and what price you are willing to pay. Yet this principle is violated regularly, often with tragic results. Leaders overreact to immediate pressures and provocations, allowing passion or truncated judgment to take them down a road that will confront them with a terrible dilemma: they cannot afford to lose, yet the price of victory is more than they can pay.

Once your purpose is clear, you need a game plan: a strategy for achieving your purpose. In sports, business, or any other competitive arena, if you think harder and better than your adversaries do, you usually win. Sam Walton entered a mature and crowded retail industry, dominated by big national players such as Sears and JCPenney with better experience, scale, and financial resources than Walton could hope to match. He bested his competitors with a simple but powerful game plan: cut costs, sell for less, offer a money-back guarantee, and go where your competitors aren't. The competition owned the cities and suburbs, so Walton gradually built his empire in rural America. Only when Wal-Mart had become a retail juggernaut did he invade the cities.

Recruit and Rally Your Team

In combat, you want comrades at your side, and they need a reason to support you. To get their support, you need to cultivate relationships and offer compelling reasons for joining your team. Sometimes followers will be spontaneously so spirited that you need only stand out of their way. More often, you need to rally your troops. Knowing the group psyche is vital: rallying constituents involves making an offer so attractive that they are eager to sign up. Such an offer needs to respond to five vital questions: What is the larger purpose of the enterprise? What makes this effort worthwhile? What is the personal meaning for each individual? (What's in it for me?) What is my role? and Will we succeed?

Steve Jobs consistently demonstrated mastery of this process, as when he recruited John Sculley from Pepsi to Apple by asking him if he'd rather sell soda or change the world. Sam Walton was an astute judge of people who drew them in with his warm, folksy touch. Even as his company grew, he stayed connected—visiting stores, talking to customers and sales clerks, asking for their ideas and suggestions. His common touch helped maintain a positive, almost warm and fuzzy image for Wal-Mart in the minds of employees and consumers, an image that only began to dissipate after Walton's death.

Build and Leverage a Power Base

No warrior wants to go into battle without the resources to win. In the old days, warriors needed physical weapons—swords, lances, bows, and the like. The modern warrior leader needs social and institutional power. Four power assets are paramount: position, allies, organization, and resources.

The power of position lets generals outrank colonels, which gives them more authority, visibility, and access to other powerful players. Allies are a second vital source of power. Smart leaders understand that they need friends. The solitary warrior, the courageous and indomitable hero, is deeply rooted in legend, myth, and movies, the central figure in many of the stories we read or watch. In film, one individual often defeats an army, fulfilling a deep hope we all share: that with skill, courage, and luck, one person can change the world. In the real world, solitary warriors usually lose, outnumbered and overwhelmed by opponents who mobilize a larger force.

Allies are all the more potent when they are welded into an effective organization or a tightly knit team. A small army can easily defeat a much larger mob. Teams and organizations are tools—sometimes very powerful tools—in the hands of anyone who can control them. Larger organizations are typically more powerful than smaller ones, because they can do more things and have more resources. But size can breed complexity and unmanageability. A fast and heroic horse may be invaluable, or useless, depending on how well you can ride it. Sam Walton demonstrated how a smaller, nimble competitor could outmaneuver and eventually overwhelm much larger competitors. The final power asset is resources—things that you own and control that give you leverage. Money, land, and a variety of physical assets can all augment leaders' ability to achieve their ends.

A CASE EXAMPLE: LOIS PAYNE

Suppose that you are a sales manager, and Lois Payne has worked in your unit for eight years. Like most employees, she has strengths and weaknesses. She meets her sales targets, and her customers like her, but she is not a top performer and can be difficult to work with. Usually friendly and charming, she nods when you make requests or offer suggestions. But then she seems to ignore your input; she's fiercely independent and likes to do things her way.

Payne tells you that she has received a job offer from a competitor that would give her a significant pay bump. She says she'll stay if you match the other offer, give her a new company car, and increase her expense account. You don't want to lose her, but she's asking for more than you think she merits. If you met her demands, she'd be earning more than your top sales-people who are significantly more productive than she is.

The job offer is real, but you suspect that Payne is bluffing and doesn't really want to leave. She's familiar with your company's product line and her current customer base, and she'd have a fairly steep learning curve at the new job. You're comfortable telling her that she's a very valuable member of the team but that you're not able to make a counteroffer at this point.

Meanwhile, one of Payne's customers has written to your boss, the sales VP, saying he knows about her job offer and might have to change vendors if she leaves. Your boss doesn't know Payne well, but your company is still recovering from the business downturn of recent years. After hearing from the customer, your boss sends you an email telling you to "figure out a way to keep her." It doesn't help that your relationship with your boss has been strained in recent months because he thinks your group should be doing better on customer retention. In light of the ideas in this chapter, how might you handle this situation?

Start by asking yourself what you're up against: Does this situation call for a warrior or a peacemaker? If you choose to become a warrior and go to battle, who is your opponent? What would constitute a win? It's easier to see costs than benefits in going to war with your boss, but you might be tempted to do battle with Payne. You suspect that she orchestrated the customer note that's adding to your problems with your boss, and you might feel that her political maneuvering is unacceptable and insubordinate. If you choose to go down the warrior path, though, remember that passion without discipline can lead to ruin. What's your goal? How well do you know your opponent? If she's politically smart, as the case hints she may be, might you start a war that costs more than it's worth? What's your strategy? Are there allies or resources you need in order to increase your chances of success? Unless you have good answers to these questions, a battle with Lois Payne could turn into the kind of self-destructive mistake that Michael Eisner made in battling Steve Jobs.

Contemplating questions like these might convince you that this is a better time to become a peacemaker. You're enmeshed in a three-way conflict without an obvious solution—unless you can orchestrate a meeting of the minds. But there's reason for optimism about a win-win solution. What if you could find a way to retain Lois Payne at a price you can afford while also improving your relationship with her and your boss? How might you go about this? Our guidelines for peacemakers counsel starting with patience: plan to spend the time needed to orchestrate a solution. The second guideline—listen and inquire—suggests spending time with both Lois and your boss (in person if possible), making sure that you understand their concerns, interests, and feelings. Ideally, this will help you strengthen your relationship with each of them and give you a clearer sense of what solutions might be workable. Payne has framed all her demands in financial terms, but you might learn, for example, that there are other, noneconomic incentives she would value.

The third guideline says to engage the parties in working on the issue. You could begin in your meetings with each of them. As you hear from Lois and your boss about their perceptions, you could ask "What if . . . ?" and "What about . . . ?" questions to test directions for coming up with solutions. You might also engage allies to assist. If, for example, you know that some of your salespeople have a good relationship with Lois, you could encourage them to talk to her, both to learn more about her thinking and to nudge her thinking in a productive direction.

A process like this does not guarantee a particular outcome. Lois Payne may stay or may wind up moving on. But you will know that you have done your best to understand what's at stake and to lead the parties toward a resolution that makes sense to everyone.

CONCLUSION

Conflict is intrinsic to leadership and can be a barrier that prevents leaders from achieving their dreams, particularly when they fear it or handle it badly. But in the hands of gifted leaders, conflict can also be a powerful lever for change. Sometimes conflict burns too hot, and leaders need to be peacemakers who find ways to lower the flame. Listening, engaging others, and depersonalizing the conflict all help to do this. In other situations, leaders need to be warriors who turn up the heat to increase their chances of success or to get people's attention and involvement in the issues at hand. But before going to war, leaders need to be sure they know what they hope to achieve, and have a strategy and tools that offer a reasonable prospect for success.

PART 5

Symbolic Leadership

Symbolic leaders see an ambiguous world in which meaning is created rather than given. They follow a consistent set of scripts and rituals to take advantage of the interpretive opportunities and challenges they encounter.

- They lead by example.
- They use symbols to unite and inspire followers.
- They interpret experience.
- They develop and communicate a hopeful vision.
- They tell stories.
- They convene rituals and ceremonies.
- They respect and use history.

The Leader as Magician

L eaders can create organizations with well-designed structures, progres-sive people policies, and well-orchestrated political dynamics, yet still be missing a key ingredient. Deep down, people want to find meaning in both life and work. The lenses of structure, people, and politics are all vital, yet by themselves may still leave an organization empty of soul and spirit. The symbolic frame can fill the gap and spiritually bond an organization and its people in a shared destiny. Symbols cluster to form culture, the shared patterns that define "our way of doing things" for a group or organization. Consider a well-known business example.

WD-40 is a staple in four of five American households. Scientists invented it in 1953 to prevent water damage and corrosion to a component of the Atlas Rocket. They mixed thirty-nine batches of test ingredients in a bathtub before arriving at their Eureka moment. The fortieth batch was a triumph, christened Water Displacement Forty, or WD-40. The ingredients, like recipes for Kentucky Fried Chicken or Coca-Cola, remain a closely guarded secret. WD-40's mystique has bred a cult around the product and its possibilities. Users have discovered unique uses for WD-40, including keeping squirrels off bird feeders, freeing tongues stuck to metal on cold winter days, coating bait to attract fish, breaking in baseball gloves, and removing pythons stuck under bus carriages.

In many ways, the culture of the WD-40 company is even more interesting than its product. "Through folklore, warriors, ceremony [and] meaningful work . . . a tribal culture is formed and becomes a self-sustaining place where people want to stay and grow."[1] Employees and executives are tribe members and live by the motto, "We work hard and learn a lot along the way. We take our work seriously but not ourselves."[2] This mantra is reflected in corporate gatherings worldwide, where tribe members play, dance, sing, and engage in riotous competitive contests.

Values bond the company together. John Barry, the CEO for many years, made this very clear: "Values, over the long haul, are more important than performance."[3] He likened values to the bank that channels a river. He saw such values as "dignity and respect for the individual" or "do the right thing" as written reminders that needed to be laced into everyday conversation to highlight expected behavior.

Another value is creating positive memories of problems solved using the company's products. Barry championed memories as the real stuff of life, "the last things that go with us in the box."[4] As a leader, he considered one of his chief duties to be creating lasting memories for other tribe members.

WD-40 is not alone in building success on a base of symbols and culture. To Herb Kelleher, who built Southwest Airlines into one of America's most successful airlines, the intangibles drive a business. For Tony Hsieh, it's a culture of happiness that generates the creativity and motivation that delivers Zappos's extraordinary levels of customer satisfaction. The late Mary Kay of Mary Kay Cosmetics relied on pink Cadillacs, diamond bumblebees, and elaborate ceremonies to create a "you can do it" spirit in the company's female sales force. Howard Schultz of Starbucks demonstrated that the revitalization of neglected cultural values and practices can pull a company out of a downward spiral. This chapter uses the story of Schultz and Starbucks to show the power of symbolic leadership in reweaving the threads of culture.

CULTURAL REVIVAL AT STARBUCKS

As he sat at his kitchen table early one morning in February 2007, Starbucks chairman and former CEO Howard Schultz was enveloped in the gloom of the Seattle weather outside his window. Until recently, his company had enjoyed extraordinary growth and profitability, but now it was showing signs of decline. Customers were spending less, growth was slowing, and the share price had plunged by more than 40 percent. When he visited individual stores, Schultz felt that "something intrinsic to the Starbucks brand was missing. An aura. A spirit. At first, I couldn't put my finger on it. No one thing was sapping our stores of a certain soul. Rather the unintended consequences resulting from the absence of several things that had distinguished our brand were, I feared, silently deflating it."[5]

The Memo

Schultz began to organize his thoughts on a yellow legal pad in a handwritten memo titled "The Commoditization of the Starbucks Experience." In it, he noted recent technical advances that were undercutting key cultural values and ways. Automatic espresso machines increased speed, consistency, and service, but eroded the mystique of the barista as a key element in the Starbucks aura of theater and romance. Sealed bags kept coffee fresher, but customers could no longer enjoy the experience and aroma of seeing or smelling it as it was ground. Streamlining and standardizing store design gained efficiencies of scale but sacrificed some of the "cozy coffee bar" ambience of the past.

Schultz ended the memo with a heartfelt statement: "We desperately need to get back to the core and make the changes necessary to evoke the heritage, the tradition, and the passion that we all have for the true Starbucks Experience."[6]

The Uproar

Schultz intended the memo as confidential food for thought for key executives, but, to his chagrin, someone leaked it. As it went viral across the Internet and the media, it set off a raucous debate inside the company. Some at Starbucks strongly disagreed with Schultz: Wasn't the coffee merchant the most visited retailer in the world? Others were confused or insulted. They were working hard to make the company better: Was Schultz saying they weren't doing their jobs? Still others felt that Schultz was speaking truths that needed to be told and debated.

Schultz was stunned by the leak and felt pressure to do damage control. But the memo expressed his passion for Starbucks, and he hoped it would generate a productive dialogue. Over the next several months, his concerns about the company's direction continued to grow. His heart sank when he walked into Starbucks stores and felt that they were no longer celebrating coffee. This violated his conviction that a true merchant creates magic and tells a story that envelops customers as they enter a shop. Months went by, and Schultz felt that nothing substantial was changing in the company or the stores. "Day by day my disappointment edged toward anger, and at times fear, that Starbucks was losing its chance to get back the magic."[7] By the end of the year, same-store sales started to show double-digit declines. Schultz and the Starbucks board agreed that he needed to return as CEO. When he did, in January 2008, he hit the ground running.

Barista Boot Camp

One of Schultz's first initiatives was to close all seventy-one hundred U.S. stores for an afternoon of barista reeducation. Notes on locked doors explained the purpose: "We're taking time to perfect our espresso. Great espresso requires practice. That's why we're dedicating ourselves to honing our craft."[8]

Some 135,000 baristas received a reintroduction to the magic of a Starbucks espresso. They brushed up on steaming milk to frothy foam. Beyond honing their beverage skills, baristas were reinfused with the spirit and heritage of Starbucks. The event cost an estimated $6 million, but Schultz felt that it was worth the investment for its symbolic value in reversing years of sacrificing spirit and heart to growth and profit.

Reinventing an Icon

Back at headquarters, Shultz worked on renewing roots with a playful brainstorming session for key executives. Outside consultants used the Beatles as a metaphor to generate creativity around the central questions: What does it mean to reinvent an icon? What could Starbucks learn from John, Paul, George, and Ringo about innovation? Reframing existing ideas with the Beatles metaphor helped people imagine new possibilities and find a better balance between heritage and innovation.

Leadership Summit

A week after the stores closed for barista training, Schultz convened the top two hundred Starbucks execs from around the world for a hands-on, interactive three-day leadership summit. He opened with a story from Paul

McCartney, who had said that the beginning of the end for the Beatles might have been their concert at Shea Stadium in New York, where the crowd was so big and enthusiastic that the Beatles couldn't hear their own music. The story raised a question that Schultz used to set the stage for the summit: "When did we stop hearing our own music?" In the next few days, the executives visited Seattle's most exciting retail shops and studied them from a customer's perspective. They spent hours in breakout groups chewing over a transformation agenda.

The climax was a ceremony of recommitment to the mission. Schultz talked about updating the mission in a way that would "capture the passion we have for the future and the respect we have for the past."[9] He read the preamble: "The Starbucks Mission: To inspire and nurture the human spirit—one person, one cup and one neighborhood at a time."[10]

Next up were representatives from headquarters and regions around the world, who read sections of the mission focusing on coffee, partners, customers, stores, neighborhoods, and shareholders. The reading sparked an emotional reaction that the group carried into the next room, where the statement was displayed on oversized pillars along with artifacts from the company's history. Veteran executives enthusiastically affixed their signatures on the large-scale replica of the document.

2008 Annual Meeting: Building Confidence

Thousands of investors and partners flocked into a large auditorium for the annual Starbucks shareholders' meeting in March 2008. The mood was tense and gloomy—the stock price had plummeted, and there was no positive news in sight. Schultz saw it as an opportunity to get people to renew their faith in the company. He opened with a frank acknowledgment: Starbucks's recent performance had been unacceptable. He made it clear, however, that the company would come back stronger than ever. "It's time to convince you and many other people who are not represented here, to give you all reasons to believe in Starbucks again. And that is exactly what we will do today."[11] He wasted no time in directing attention to a large black draped object beside him on stage. With dramatic flair, he unveiled a glittering copper and stainless steel appliance: a new espresso machine that no longer blocked the sight line between customer and barista. For

Schultz, the new machine solved problems of both quality and theater. A delighted crowd roared as a barista, with panache, prepared an espresso for Schultz.

He then introduced more crowd pleasers, including a Rewards Card and an interactive website. The final initiatives focused on coffee. The crowd got a chance to taste a new, milder brew, Pike's Peak Roast. They saw a demonstration of the showy, high-tech Clover coffee maker, a machine that Schultz extolled as replicating the virtues of French-press coffee. Schultz closed the meeting to enthusiastic shareholder applause.

The Galvanizing Extravaganza

After the 2008 Wall Street meltdown, Starbucks lost $7 million for the third quarter and had to close six hundred stores. Articles in the business press opined that Starbucks's best days were behind it. Schultz was getting advice to sell the company or to save a few million dollars by roasting slightly cheaper coffee because "no one would know." He was also under pressure to cancel the expensive biennial leadership conference. Did Starbucks really need a $30 million managers' meeting? The answer was clear to Schultz. In his mind, there was no better time for a company rally.

In October 2008, ten thousand regional, district, and store managers streamed into New Orleans, a city struggling to come back after Hurricane Katrina. One of the city's legendary marching bands greeted them at the airport. On the way to their hotels, they saw blue and green banners hanging from streetlamps and boldly declaring, BELIEVE.

The convention center itself was huge, large enough to accommodate four huge walkthrough displays, each organized around a different theme: coffee, customers, partners, and stores. Starbucks partners could experience dramatic scenes of coffee's journey from soil to cup. "Each gallery was interactive. It was emotional. It was multisensory. It was storytelling."[12]

The ten thousand Starbucks people were there for more than business or learning; they also were there to roll up their sleeves and help New Orleans rebuild. Work teams flooded the city—planting trees, refurbishing and painting old homes, and erecting new ones. T-shirts bore one word, ONWARD, a signal to themselves and to the people of New Orleans that troubled times require moving ahead with hope and faith. "In times of adversity and change, we really discover who we are and what we are made of."[13]

At the closing session in the New Orleans Arena, Schultz acknowledged the daunting challenges facing the company, but also offered a message of hope. Schultz, like his fellow business legend Steve Jobs, liked to give an audience more than they expect. The dazzling surprise was U2's lead singer, Bono, a rock star and humanitarian who had helped raise more than $2 million for post-Katrina relief. The crowd cheered wildly as Bono joined Schultz onstage and began to talk about partnering with Starbucks to combat poverty and AIDS in Africa. "Great companies," he said, "will be the ones that find a way to have and hold onto their values while chasing their profits, and brand values will converge to create a new business model that unites commerce and compassion. The heart and the wallet."[14]

The crowd's reaction to Bono's speech reaffirmed the conference's theme of "Believe: in the heritage and future of our company." Then Schultz ended the gathering: "Please remember what you have experienced here. Remember how you felt. And when you get back, please do not be a bystander . . . Do not allow the pressures of the day to in any way erode the emotion, the feeling, and the power of 10,000 that you each experienced in the last few days."[15]

■ ■ ■

Schultz's package of symbolic initiatives helped to refocus Starbucks's strategy and reenergize its people. The New Orleans meeting came just as Starbucks was hitting the bottom of a two-year slide. From losses in late 2008, Starbucks rebounded to record revenues ($10.7 billion) and profits ($1.4 billion) two years later, while retaining its place on *Fortune*'s list of the one hundred best companies to work for and expanding its efforts to become greener and provide more support to coffee growers. One analyst called it the most remarkable turnaround he had ever witnessed. Since then, Starbucks has continued its upward spiral in growth and profits. In the second quarter of 2012, the company's earnings were up 15 percent, and Schultz received *Fortune* magazine's award as Businessperson of the Year.

Reviewing the Cultural Threads of the Starbucks Story

Culture is not easy to see when you are enmeshed in it. Pared to the bone, culture is "the way we do things around here" or "what keeps the herd moving roughly in the same direction." Schultz was able to step back and view the Starbucks culture by focusing on the symbolic threads that intertwine to form a meaningful enterprise. These include history, values, heroes, rituals, ceremonies, stories, and a cultural network of informal players.

In reweaving the cultural tapestry of Starbucks, Schultz relied on the mystical power of all these symbolic threads.

THE WAYS OF MAGIC: HOW SYMBOLIC LEADERS WORK

Leaders like Howard Schultz lead through both actions and words; they interpret experience to impart meaning and purpose through phrases of beauty and passion. Franklin D. Roosevelt reassured a nation in the midst of its deepest economic depression that "the only thing we have to fear is fear itself." Symbolic leadership begins with the leader's deeply rooted faith and passion. Schultz had had a successful career selling, first, copier machines and then kitchen products. But he only fell in love when he savored his first cup of espresso and was enveloped by the harmonizing ritual in Milan. Armed with that passion, Schultz built a great company by intuitively employing the ways of magic that come naturally to symbolic leaders.

Symbolic Leaders Respect and Use History

If leaders assume that history starts with their arrival, they typically misread their circumstances and alienate their constituents. Wise leaders attend to history and link their initiatives to the values, stories, and heroes of the past. When the Starbucks founders nixed Schultz's vision of recreating the Italian espresso experience in America, he started his own business, *Il Giornale*. It was successful, but his instincts told him that he wanted the power of Starbucks's history and the "mystical quality" of its name. Starbuck was the first mate of the whaling ship *Pequod* in Herman Melville's classic sea story *Moby Dick*. Schultz eventually persuaded the founders to sell him what was then a tiny, highly successful chain of stores in Seattle.

Symbolic Leaders Interpret Experience

In a world of uncertainty and ambiguity, a key function of symbolic leadership is to offer plausible and hopeful interpretations of experience. President John F. Kennedy channeled youthful exuberance into the Peace Corps and other initiatives with his stirring inaugural challenge: "Ask not what your country can do for you; ask what you can do for your country." When Howard Schultz began to build his fledgling company, many people told him he was crazy to think that Americans would ever spend $1.50 for a cup of espresso. But to Schultz, Starbucks was more than coffee. It was a "third place" between home and work, "a social yet personal environment where people can connect with others and reconnect with themselves."[16] In reframing the meaning and possibilities of something as mundane as a coffee shop, Schultz exemplified his view of what great merchants do: "We take something ordinary and infuse it with emotion and meaning, and then we tell its story over and over again, often without saying a word."[17] Having a cup of coffee at Starbucks is "enjoying the Starbucks Experience."

Symbolic Leaders Develop and Communicate a Hopeful Vision

One powerful way in which a leader can interpret experience is by distilling and disseminating a persuasive and hopeful image of the future. A vision needs to address both the challenges of the present and the hopes and values of followers.

Where does such vision come from? One view is that leaders create a vision and then persuade others to accept it. If we look at Howard Schultz, we see that the reality is more subtle. Schultz didn't know he wanted to be in the coffee business until he tasted his first cup of Starbucks coffee, and his image of coffee shops as places for connection and community only began to crystallize as he toured espresso bars in Italy. Schultz's magic lay in his intuitive ability to assemble a vision from bits and pieces that were already there in a scattered and inchoate form.

Leadership is a two-way street. No amount of charisma or rhetorical skill can sell a vision that speaks only to the person selling it. Leaders play a critical role in articulating a shared dream by distilling a unique, personal blend of history, poetry, passion, and courage.

Symbolic Leaders Lead by Example

These leaders demonstrate their commitment and courage by plunging into the fray. In taking risks and holding nothing back, they reassure and inspire others. In Chapter Six, we saw Anne Mulcahy take the top job at Xerox in 2001, when the building was burning and few thought she had much chance of putting out the fire. Her financial advisers told her that bankruptcy was the only choice. But she was determined to save the company she loved, and became a tireless, visible icon working to get the support she needed to make Xerox a success. When Howard Schultz returned as Starbucks's CEO after an eight-year hiatus, he threw himself back into the business he loved—not because he had to, but because he believed that his instincts and example would provide the spark the company needed. His passion and resolve communicated to others that Starbucks could and would reclaim its soul.

Symbolic Leaders Tell Stories

Howard Schultz has described Starbucks as a "living legacy" to his father. The stories he tells about growing up poor in a subsidized housing project in Brooklyn, New York, shape his values and the culture he has built at Starbucks. He has never forgotten the time in 1961 when he was seven years old and his dad broke his ankle at work. Fred Schultz hadn't liked his job as a truck driver for a diaper service, but now he couldn't work and had no income or health benefits. Howard Schultz felt that his father deserved better. Even when Starbucks was losing money in its early days, Schultz insisted on providing health care coverage and stock options for employees. At times when Starbucks's business slumped, investors or analysts sometimes pressured him to goose the bottom line by cutting the health care benefits. That suggestion was always a nonstarter for Schultz. In his mind, a company can be great only if it provides the benefits and pride that his father never experienced.

Stories abound in successful companies. Ritz-Carlton is renowned for its platinum standard of guest service: "Ladies and Gentlemen serving Ladies and Gentlemen." Employees carry a list of "service values" with them while at work, and focus every day on a value selected for special attention. During frequent "lineups," cross-sections of employees meet in a ritual to reinforce the importance of guest service and to hear and tell stories of employees who have gone out of their way to satisfy guests. For example, a family that had stayed at a Ritz-Carlton arrived home to a crisis: their toddler's treasured stuffed animal, JoJo, had been left behind. They sent an emergency message to the hotel, which put out an all-points bulletin. Housekeeping searched the room and the laundry. Bellmen, concierges, and other staff member scoured the premises. Once JoJo was finally tracked down, a creative Ritz-Carlton staffer took him around the hotel and photographed him in assorted locales—the kitchen, the lobby, a guest room, and so on. She then packaged JoJo with the photos and a note indicating that he had had a wonderful time and made many new friends during his stay. The little girl was thrilled. Her delighted parents may never stay at any other hotel.

Stories succeed because they are truer than true. We want to believe them rather than to scrutinize their historical validity or empirical support.

Symbolic Leaders Convene Rituals and Ceremonies

Rituals and ceremonies are special times in the life of a group or organization. During such occasions, people swap stories, renew ties to one another, and recommit to cultural values. Schultz relied heavily on ritual and ceremony to restore the company's ties to its cultural roots and vitality.

Recall that his first step was to close Starbucks stores for a "reeducation of baristas." Baristas are Starbucks's front line, with direct contact with customers, what Jan Carlzon of SAS called "The Moment of Truth."[18] Schultz did not conceive of the event as a skill session, but rather as an opportunity to get baristas to fall in love with coffee again, to regain passion for every cup they served.

Once the front line was energized, Schultz convened a series of special events, beginning at the top and building to the New Orleans extravaganza involving ten thousand store managers. All these occasions focused on renewing the soul and spirit of the company.

CONCLUSION

Symbolic leaders infuse magic into organizations through their artistic focus on history, shared values, heroes, ritual, ceremony, and stories, and serve as icons who embody a group's values and spirit. People yearn for meaningful work in organizations that unite commerce and compassion, the wallet and the heart. They want to make a difference. They can find what they are looking for in organizations with a vibrant and cohesive culture that breathes meaning, life, and hope into everyday doings.

Seeking Soul in Teams

Teams often fall short because they come together rationally but not spiritually. Uncommon spirit—or soul—is often the key ingredient of wildly successful teams or "hot groups."[1] Lockheed's Skunk Works is one famous example of an autonomous team unhampered by bureaucracy; it built America's first jet fighter as well as the legendary U-2 surveillance aircraft. Another is Steve Jobs's band of "Pirates," swashbucklers and rebels who seceded from the main Apple campus to work on special projects: "It's better to be a pirate than join the Navy."[2] But there are many others. Breakthroughs in medical research rarely happen without a team of scientists deeply committed to finding a cure for a deadly disease. The sports world is riddled with stories of athletic teams playing above their heads to snatch victory against overwhelming odds.

Leadership is often viewed as the work of extraordinary individuals, but in great groups, leadership is almost always shared and fluid. Leadership initially focuses on assembling individuals with the right stuff and building powerful cultural bonds that inspire and sustain team members through the ups and downs of challenging work. As a widely reported recent example, one of these tightly knit teams, Red Squadron of Seal Team Six, shot and killed Osama bin Laden to end an exhaustive ten-year effort to avenge the death and devastation of 9/11.

This was not the team's first covert mission, and it would not be their last. They are a permanent operational unit bonded by a cultural fabric woven over time. "They are bound together by sworn oaths and the obligations of

119

their brotherhood."[3] Red Squadron has learned from the history of previous missions, both successes and failures. Stories carry its lore. Members have their own language. Ritual and ceremony reaffirm the team's sacred and secret covenant. The team acknowledges heroic actions within the tight circle, but secrets stay inside. For example, no one but the members of Red Squadron will ever know who fired the two rounds that killed bin Laden.[4]

Prescriptions for building such extraordinary teamwork often emphasize the intensive training and structural precision of groups like the Seals, and they only hint at the deeper symbolic secret of how groups and teams reach a state of grace and peak performance. Former Visa CEO Dee Hock captured the heart of the issue: "In the field of group endeavor, you will see incredible events in which the group performs far beyond the sum of its individual talents. It happens in the symphony, in the ballet, in the theater, in sports, and equally in business. It is easy to recognize and impossible to define. It is a mystique. It cannot be achieved without immense effort, training, and cooperation, but effort, training, and cooperation alone rarely create it."[5]

Accounts of team success often lack the fine-grained nuance needed to portray the rich symbolic tapestry at the heart of such extraordinary performance. In the provocative case of Red Squadron, most details of the team's culture are shrouded in secrecy. In other examples, observers miss the subtle cultural clues that might help leaders get better at creating cohesive, high-performing teams in their place of work. But occasionally someone tells a story of teamwork with sufficient detail and time span to provide tangible hints and guidelines for achieving magic.

THE EAGLE GROUP: REASONS FOR SUCCESS

The Soul of a New Machine is Tracy Kidder's dazzling yearlong account of a small group of engineers at Data General who, in the 1970s, created a new computer in record time.[6] Despite scant resources and limited support, the Eagle Group outperformed all other Data General divisions to produce a new state-of-the-art machine. After accomplishing the mission, the group disbanded, and the members left to pursue other interests. The technology is now antiquated, but lessons from how the team pulled it off are as current and useful as ever.

Why did the Eagle Group succeed? Were the project members extraordinarily talented? Not really. Each was highly skilled, but there were equally talented engineers working on other Data General projects. Were team members treated with dignity and respect? Quite the contrary. As one engineer noted, "No one ever pats anyone on the back."[7] Instead, the group experienced what they called "mushroom management": "Put 'em in the dark, feed 'em shit, and watch 'em grow."[8] For over a year, group members jeopardized their health, their families, and their careers. Another engineer exclaimed paradoxically, "I'm flat out by definition. I'm a mess. It's terrible. It's a lot of fun."[9]

Were financial rewards a motivating factor? Group members agreed collectively that they did not work for money. Nor were they motivated by fame. Heroic efforts were rewarded neither by formal appreciation nor by official applause.

Perhaps the group's structure accounted for its success. Did the group have clear and well-coordinated roles and relationships? According to Kidder, it kept no meaningful charts, graphs, or organization tables. One of the group's engineers put it bluntly: "The whole management structure—anyone in Harvard Business School would have barfed."[10]

Can tenets of the political frame unravel the secret of the group's phenomenal performance? Perhaps group members were motivated more by power than by money: "There's a big high in here somewhere for me that I don't fully understand. Some of it's a raw power trip. The reason I work is because I win."[11] They were encouraged to circumvent formal channels to advance mission-related interests: "If you can't get what you need from some manager at your level in another department, go to his boss—that's the way to get things done."[12]

Although the structural, human resource, and political frames shed some light on the Eagle Group's success, the invisible force that gave the team its spirit and drive was a shared and cohesive culture expressed through symbols and symbolic activities that embodied the deeper aspects of the team's inner workings.

Signing Up

Joining a team involves more than a rational decision. It is a mutual choice marked by some form of ritual. In the Eagle Group, the process of becoming a member was called "signing up." New recruits were told that they were volunteering to climb Mount Everest without a rope despite lacking the "right stuff" to keep up with other climbers. When they protested that they wanted to climb Mount Everest anyway, they were advised that they would have to prove they were good enough. After the rigorous selections, one of their leaders summed up the process: "It was kind of like recruiting for a suicide mission. You're gonna die, but you're gonna die in glory."[13]

Through the signing-up ritual, an engineer became a full-fledged member of a group with a special calling and agreed to forsake family, friends, and health to accomplish the impossible. It was a sacred declaration: "I want to do this job and I'll give it my heart and soul."[14]

Leadership Diversity as a Competitive Advantage

Though nearly all the group's members were engineers, each had unique skills and made distinctive leadership contributions. Tom West, the group's official leader, was known as a talented technical debugger. He was also aloof and unapproachable, the "Prince of Darkness." Steve Wallach, the group's computer architect, was a creative maverick. Before accepting West's invitation to join the group, he went to Edson de Castro, the president of Data General, to find out precisely what he'd be working on:

> "Okay," Wallach said, "what the fuck do you want?"
> "I want a thirty-two-bit Eclipse," de Castro told him.
> "If we can do this, you won't cancel it on us?" Wallach asked.
> "You'll leave us alone?"[15]

Wallach signed up.

Leadership diversity among the group's top engineers was channeled into specialized functions. Wallach was a wunderkind who liked coming up with an esoteric idea and then trying to make it work. He created the original design. Rasala, one of his lieutenants, was a craftsman who enjoyed fixing things, working tirelessly until the last bug had been tracked down and eliminated. West, their boss, buffered the team from upper management interference and served as a group "devil." Alsing, the code writer, and his group named "Microkids" created "a synaptic language that would fuse the physical machine with the programs that would tell it what to do."[16] Rasala, Alsing's counterpart, and his group, the "Hardy Boys," built the physical circuitry.

Understandably, there was tension among these leadership roles and subgroups. Harnessing the resulting energy pulled the parts into a cohesive team.

Example, Not Command

Wallach's design generated modest coordination for Eagle's autonomous subunits. The group itself had some rules, but paid little attention to them. De Castro, the CEO, was a distant god. He was never there physically, but his presence was always felt. West, the group's official leader, rarely interfered, nor was he visible in the laboratory. He contributed by creating an almost endless series of "brushfires" so that he could inspire his staff to put them out. He had a mischievous knack for finding drama and romance in everyday routine.

Alsing and Rasala followed de Castro and West in creating ambiguity, encouraging inventiveness, and leading by example. Heroes of the moment gave inspiration and direction. Subtle and implicit signals rather than concrete and explicit guidelines or decisions held the group together and directed it toward a common purpose.

Specialized Language

Every unified group develops words, phrases, and metaphors unique to its circumstances. A specialized language both reflects and shapes a group's culture. Shared language allows team members to communicate easily, with minimal misunderstanding. To the members of the Eagle Group, for example, a *kludge* was a poor, inelegant solution—such as a machine with loose wires held together with duct tape. A *canard* was anything false. *Fundamentals* were the source of enlightened thinking. The word *realistically* typically prefaced flights of fantasy. "Give me a *core dump*" meant tell me your thoughts. A *stack overflow* meant that an engineer's memory compartments were too full, and a *one-stack-deep mind* indicated shallow thinking. *Eagle* was a label for the project; *Hardy Boys* and *Microkids* gave identity to the subgroups. Two prototype computers were named *Woodstock* and *Trixie*.

A shared language binds a group together and is a visible sign of membership. It also sets a group apart and reinforces unique values and beliefs. Asked about the Eagle Group's headquarters, West observed, "It's basically a cattle yard. What goes on here is not part of the real world." Asked for an explanation, West remarked, "Mmm-hmm. The language is different."[17]

Stories

In high-performing groups, stories keep traditions alive and provide examples to guide everyday behavior. Group lore extended and reinforced the subtle yet powerful influence of Eagle's leaders—some of them distant and remote. West's reputation as a "troublemaker" and an "excitement junkie" was conveyed through stories about the computer wars of the mid-1970s. Stories had it that when he had a particular objective in mind, he would first go upstairs to sign up senior executives. Then he went to people one at a time, telling them their bosses liked the idea and asking them to come on board: "They say, 'Ah, it sounds like you're just gonna put a bag on the side of the Eclipse,' and Tom'll give 'em his little grin and say, 'It's more than that, we're really gonna build this fucker and it's gonna be fast as greased lightning.' He tells them, 'we're gonna do it by April.'"[18]

Stories of persistence, irreverence, and creativity encouraged others to go beyond themselves, adding new exploits and tales to the Eagle Group's lore.

Humor and Play

Groups often focus single-mindedly on the task, shunning anything not directly work related. Seriousness replaces playfulness as a cardinal virtue. However, effective teams balance seriousness with play and humor. Surgical teams, cockpit crews, and many other groups have learned that joking and playful banter are essential sources of invention, attentiveness, and team spirit. Humor releases tension and helps resolve issues arising from day-to-day routines as well as from sudden emergencies.

Play among the members of the Eagle project was an innate part of the group process. When Alsing wanted the Microkids to learn how to manipulate the computer known as Trixie, he made up a game. As the Microkids came on board, he told each of them to figure out how to write a program in Trixie's assembly language. The program had to fetch and print contents of a file stored inside the computer. The Microkids went to work, learned their way around the machine, and felt great satisfaction—until Alsing's perverse sense of humor tripped them up. When they finally found the elusive file, they were greeted with the message "Access Denied." Through such play, the Microkids learned to use the computer, coalesced into a team, and practiced negotiating their new technical environment. They also learned that their playful leader valued creativity. Humor was a continuous thread as the team struggled with its formidable task. Humor often stretched the boundaries of good taste, but that too was part of the group's identity.

Ritual and Ceremony

Rituals and ceremonies are expressive occasions. As parentheses in an ordinary workday, they enclose and define special forms of behavior. What occurs on the surface is not nearly as important as the meaning communicated behind and beneath. Despite the stereotype of narrowly task-focused engineers with little time for anything nonrational, the Eagle Group understood the importance of symbolic goings-on. From the beginning, the leaders encouraged ritual and ceremony.

For example, Rasala, head of the Hardy Boys, established a rule requiring that changes in the boards of the prototype be updated each morning. This allowed efforts to be coordinated formally. More important, the daily update was a ritualistic occasion for informal communication, bantering, and gaining a sense of the whole. The engineers disliked the daily procedure, so Rasala changed it to once a week—on Saturday. He made it a point always to be there himself.

Eagle's leaders met regularly, but their meetings focused more on symbolic issues than on substance. "'We could be in a lot of trouble here,' West might say, referring to some current problem. And Wallach, Rasala or Alsing would reply, 'You mean you could be in a lot of trouble, right, Tom?' It was Friday, they were going home soon, and relaxing. They could half forget that they would be coming back to work tomorrow."[19] Friday afternoon is a customary time to wind down and relax. Honoring such a tradition was all the more important for a group whose members often worked all week and then all weekend. West made himself available to anyone who wanted to chat. Near the end of the day, before hurrying home, he would lean back in his chair with his office door open.

In addition to recurring rituals, the Eagle Group convened intermittent ceremonies to raise their spirits and reinforce their sense of shared mission. Toward the end of the project, Alsing instigated a ceremony to trigger a burst of renewed energy for the final push. The festivities called attention to the values of creativity, hard work, and teamwork. A favorite pretext for parties was presentation of the Honorary Microcoder Awards that Alsing and the Microkids instituted. Not to be outdone, the Hardy Boys cooked up the PAL Awards (named for the programmable array logic chips used in the machines). The first was presented after work at a local establishment called the Cain Ridge Saloon.

The same values and spirit were reinforced again and again in a continued cycle of celebratory events:

> Chuck Holland [Alsing's main submanager] handed out his own special awards to each member of the Microteam, the Under Extraordinary Pressure Awards. They looked like diplomas. There was one for Neal Firth, "who gave us a computer before the hardware guys did," and one to Betty Shanahan, "for putting up with a bunch of creepy guys." After dispensing the Honorary Microcoder Awards to almost every possible candidate, the Microteam instituted the All-Nighter Award. The first of these went to Jim Guyer, the citation ingeniously inserted under the clear plastic coating of an insulated coffee cup.[20]

The Contribution of Informal Cultural Players

Alsing was the main organizer and instigator of parties. He was also the Eagle Group's conscience and nearly everyone's confidant. For a time when he was in college, Alsing had wanted to become a psychologist. He adopted that sort of role now. He kept track of his team's technical progress, but was more visible as the spiritual director of the Microteam, and often of the entire Eclipse Group. Fairly early in the project, Chuck Holland had complained, "Alsing's hard to be a manager for, because he goes around you a lot and tells your people to do something else." But Holland also conceded, "The good thing about him is that you can go and talk to him. He's more of a regular guy than most managers."[21]

Every group or organization has a "priest" or "priestess" who ministers to spiritual needs. Informally, these people hear confessions, give blessings, maintain traditions, encourage ceremonies, and intercede in matters of gravest importance. Alsing did all these things and, like the tribal priest, acted as a counterpart to and interpreter of the intentions of the chief:

> West warned him several times, "If you get too close to the people who work for you, Alsing, you're gonna get burned." But West didn't interfere, and he soon stopped issuing warnings.
>
> One evening, while alone with West in West's office, Alsing said: "Tom, the kids think you're an ogre. You don't even say hello to them."
>
> West smiled and replied, "You're doing fine, Alsing."[22]

The duties of Rosemarie Seale, the group's secretary, also went well beyond formal boundaries. If Alsing was the priest, she was the mother superior. She did all the usual secretarial chores—answering the phones, preparing documents, and constructing budgets—but she found particular joy in serving as a kind of blessed den mother who solved minor crises that arose almost daily. When new members came on, it was Seale who worried about finding them a desk and some pencils. She liked the job, she said, because she felt that she was contributing something of real significance to the project.

BUILDING A SOULFUL TEAM

The experiences of the Eagle Group, Skunk Works, and Red Squadron are unique. But the leadership principles behind their success can be applied to teams anywhere. After extensive research on high-performing groups, Peter Vaill concluded that spirit was at the core of every group he studied. Members of such groups consistently "felt the spirit," a feeling essential to the meaning and value of their work.[23] Warren Bennis could have been writing about the Eagle Group, Skunk Works, or Red Squadron when he concluded, "All Great Groups believe that they are on a mission from God, that they could change the world, make a dent in the universe. They are obsessed with their work. It becomes not a job but a fervent quest. That belief is what brings the necessary cohesion and energy to their work."[24]

CONCLUSION

From the Eagle Group's experience and from what we know about Lockheed's Skunk Works and Team Six's Red Squadron, we have distilled tenets that can guide leaders in building great teams.

- How someone becomes a group member is important.
- Diverse leadership supports a team's competitive advantage.
- Example, not command, holds a team together.
- A specialized language fosters cohesion and commitment.
- Stories carry history and values and reinforce group identity.
- Humor and play reduce tension and encourage creativity.
- Ritual and ceremony lift spirits and reinforce values.
- Informal cultural players make contributions disproportionate to their formal role.
- Soul is the secret of success.

Team building at its heart is a spiritual undertaking. The leader's work is both a search for the spirit within and the creation of a community of believers united by shared faith and culture. Peak performance emerges as a team discovers its soul.

PART 6

Improving Leadership Practice

Leaders see more and get more done when they develop and use key leadership capacities:

- They reframe on the fly and use alternative scripts to guide their thinking and action in critical situations.
- They know the "shape of their leadership kite," build on their strengths, and find ways to compensate for blind spots.
- They employ a holistic, multiframe approach to change.
- They root their leadership in a deep sense of self and values.
- They weave their own story and that of their organization into a compelling narrative that provides a shared image of where they are and where they need to go.

Reframing in Action

Most leadership challenges can be framed in more than one way, and every turn of the kaleidoscope offers a different image of the problems and possibilities. Put yourself in the shoes of Olivia Martin, headed to work for your first day in a new job. Your company has transferred you to Atlanta to lead a customer service unit. It's a big promotion, with a substantial increase in pay and responsibility. You know it won't be easy. You're inheriting a department with a reputation for slow, mediocre service. Senior leadership blames the rigid, bureaucratic style of your predecessor, Jack Davis. Davis is moving to another job, but the company asked him to stay on for a week to help with your transition. One potential sticking point is that he hired most of the staff. Many may still feel loyal to him.

When you arrive, your welcome from Rosa Garcia, the department secretary, feels frosty. As you walk into your new office, you see Davis behind the desk in a conversation with three other staff members. You say hello, and he responds by saying, "Didn't the secretary tell you that we're in a meeting right now? If you'll wait outside, I'll be able to see you in about an hour."

You're in the glare of the spotlight, and the audience eagerly awaits your response. As Olivia Martin, what would you do? If you feel threatened or attacked—as many of us would—your feelings will push you toward either fight or flight. Fighting back and escalating the conflict is risky and could make things worse. Backing away or fleeing could suggest that you are too emotional or not tough enough.

This is a classic example of a leader's nightmare: an unexpected situation that threatens to explode in your face. Davis's greeting is stealthily designed to throw you off stride and put you in a bind. It would be easy to feel trapped and powerless or to do something rash and regrettable. Either way, Davis wins and you lose.

The leadership lenses suggest another set of possibilities. They offer the advantage of multiple angles to size up the situation. What's really going on here? What options do you have? What script does the situation suggest? How might you reinterpret the scene to create a more effective scenario? In tough situations, reframing is a powerful tool for generating possibilities other than fight or flight. Keep your Leadership Orientations Profile (Appendix) in mind as you explore different scenarios for avoiding the trap that Jack Davis has set for you.

An immediate question facing you, as Olivia Martin, is whether to respond on the spot to Davis's provocation, or to buy time. If you're at a loss or you're tempted to do something you might regret, take time to "go to the balcony." Try to rise above the confusion of the moment long enough to get a better angle and develop a workable strategy. Even better, though, is to find an effective response in the moment.

Each of the frames generates its own alternative scenarios. Depending on how you apply it, each frame could work well or poorly. Success depends on the script you choose and on your skill and artistry in execution. We describe different scenarios Martin could choose, showing that each of the four lenses can produce either effective or ineffective reactions.

A Structural Scenario

A structural scenario casts leaders as authorities responsible for clarifying goals, attending to the link between structure and environment, and developing a set of roles and relationships appropriate to what needs to be done. Without authority and a workable structure, people become unsure about what they are supposed to be doing. The result is confusion, frustration, and conflict. With the right structure, the organization can achieve its goals, and individuals can see their role in the big picture.

Structural leaders focus on tasks, facts, and logic rather than personality and emotions. They see most people problems as stemming from structural flaws, not personal limits or defects. Structural leaders are not rigidly authoritarian and do not attempt to solve every problem by issuing orders (though doing so is sometimes appropriate). Instead, leaders rely on legitimate authority and try to design and implement a process or architectural form appropriate to the circumstances.

You may wonder what structure has to do with a personal confrontation, but the structural scenario in the box can be scripted to generate a variety of responses.

Here's one example:

Davis: Didn't the secretary tell you that we're in a meeting right now? If you'll wait outside, I'll be able to see you in about an hour.

Martin: My appointment as manager of this office began at nine this morning. This is now my job and my office . . . and you're sitting behind my desk. Either you relinquish the desk immediately, or I will call headquarters and report you for insubordination.

Davis: I was asked to stay on the job for one more week to try to help you learn the ropes. Frankly, I doubt that you're ready for this job, but you don't seem to want any help.

Martin: I repeat, I am now in charge. Let me also remind you that headquarters assigned you to stay this week to assist me. I expect you to carry out that order. If you don't, I will submit a letter for your file detailing your lack of cooperation. Now, *(firmly)* I want my desk.

Davis: Well, we were working on important office business, but since the princess here is more interested in giving orders than in getting work done, let's move our meeting down to your office, Joe. Enjoy the desk!

In this exchange, Olivia places heavy emphasis on her formal authority and the chain of command. By invoking her superiors and her legitimate authority, she takes charge and gets Davis to back down, but at a price. She risks long-term tension with her new subordinates, who surely feel awkward during this combative encounter. They may see their new boss as autocratic and dangerous.

There are better options. Here's another example of how Martin might exercise her authority:

Davis: Didn't the secretary tell you that we're in a meeting right now? If you'll wait outside, I'll be able to see you in about an hour.

Martin: She didn't mention it, and I don't want to interrupt important work, but we also need to set some priorities and work out an agenda for

---

(continued)

the day anyway. Jack, have you developed a plan for how you and I can get to work on the transition?

Davis: We can meet later on, after I get through some pressing business.

Martin: The pressing business is just the kind of thing I need to learn about as the new manager here. What issues are you discussing?

Davis: How to keep the office functioning when the new manager is not ready for the job.

Martin: Well, I have a lot to learn, but I feel up to it. With your help, I think we can have a smooth and productive changeover. How about if you continue your meeting and I just sit in as an observer? Then, Jack, you and I could meet to work out a plan for how we'll handle the transition. After that, I'd like to schedule a meeting with each manager to get an individual progress report. I'd like to hear from each of you about your major customer service objectives and how you would assess your progress. Now, what were you talking about before I got here?

This time, Martin is still clear and firm in establishing her authority, but she does it without appearing harsh or dictatorial. She underscores the importance of setting priorities. She asks if Davis has a plan for making the transition productive. She emphasizes shared goals and defines a temporary role for herself as an observer. She focuses steadfastly on the task instead of on Davis's provocations. By keeping the exchange on a rational level and outlining a transition plan, she avoids escalating or submerging the conflict. She also communicates to her new staff that she has done her homework, is organized, and knows what she wants to accomplish. When she says she would like to hear their personal objectives and progress, she communicates an expectation that they will be heard, but that she is in charge.

A Human Resource Scenario

Human resource leaders believe that people are the center of any organization. If people feel that the organization is responsive to their needs and supportive of their personal goals, they will respond with commitment and loyalty. Leaders who are authoritarian or insensitive, who don't communicate effectively, or who don't care will be ineffective. The human resource leader works on behalf of both the organization and its people, seeking to serve the best interests of both.

The job of the leader is support and empowerment. Support takes a variety of forms: showing concern, listening to people's aspirations and goals, and communicating personal warmth and openness. The leader empowers through participation and inclusion, ensuring that people have the autonomy and encouragement needed to do their jobs. The approach favors listening and responsiveness.

Some people, though, go a little too far in making an effort:

Davis: Didn't the secretary tell you that we're in a meeting right now? If you'll wait outside, I'll be able to see you in about an hour.

Martin: Oh, gosh, no, she didn't. I feel terrible about interrupting your meeting. I hope I didn't offend anyone, because to me, it's really important to establish good working relationships right from the outset. While I'm waiting, is there anything I can do to help? Would anyone like a cup of coffee?

Davis: No. We'll let you know when we're finished.

Martin: Oh. Well, have a good meeting, and I'll see you in an hour.

In the effort to be friendly and accommodating, Martin is acting more like a waitress than a manager. She defuses the conflict, but her staff is likely to see their new boss as weak. She could instead capitalize on an interest in people:

Davis: Didn't the secretary tell you that we're in a meeting right now? If you'll wait outside, I'll be able to see you in about an hour.

Martin: I'm sorry if I'm interrupting, but I'm eager to get started, and I'll need all your help. *(She walks around, introduces herself, and shakes hands with each member of her new staff. Davis scowls silently.)* Jack, could we take a few minutes to talk about how we can work together on the transition, now that I'm coming in to manage the department?

(continued)

> Davis: You're not the manager yet. I was asked to stay on for a week to get you started—though, frankly, I doubt that you're ready for this job.
>
> Martin: I understand your concern, Jack. I know how committed you are to the success of the department. If I were you, I might be worried about whether I was turning my baby over to someone who wouldn't be able to take care of it. But I wouldn't be here if I didn't feel ready. I want to benefit as much as I can from your experience. Is it urgent to get on with what you were talking about, or could we take some time first to talk about how we can start working together?
>
> Davis: We have some things we need to finish.
>
> Martin: Well, as a manager, I always prefer to trust the judgment of the people who are closest to the action. I'll just sit in while you finish up, and then we can talk about how we move forward from there.

Here, Martin is unfazed and relentlessly cheerful; she avoids a battle and acknowledges Davis's perspective. When he says she is not ready for the job, she resists the temptation to counter his salvo. Instead, she recognizes his concern but calmly communicates her confidence and focus on moving ahead. She demonstrates an important skill of a human resource leader: the ability to combine advocacy with inquiry. She listens carefully to Davis, but gently stands her ground. She asks for his help while expressing confidence that she can do the job. When he says they have things to finish, she responds with the agility of a martial artist, using Davis's energy to her own advantage. She expresses part of her philosophy—she prefers to trust her staff's judgment—and positions herself as an observer, thus gaining an opportunity to learn more about her staff and the issues they are addressing. By reframing the situation, she has gotten off to a better start with Davis and is able to signal to others the kind of people-oriented leader she intends to be.

A Political Scenario

Political leaders believe that it is essential to recognize differences and deal with conflict. Inside and outside any organization, a variety of interest groups, each with its own agenda, compete for scarce resources. There is never enough to give all parties what they want, so there will always be struggles.

> The job of the leader is to recognize major constituencies, develop ties to their leadership, and manage conflict as productively as possible. Above all, leaders need to build a power base and use power wisely. They can't give every group everything it wants, but they can create arenas where groups can negotiate differences and come up with a reasonable compromise. They also need to work at articulating what everyone has in common. It is wasteful for people to expend energy fighting each other when there are plenty of external adversaries to battle. Any group that doesn't have its act together internally tends to get trounced by outsiders.

Some leaders translate the political approach as meaning that they should manage by intimidation and manipulation. It sometimes works, but the risks are high. Here's an example:

> *Davis:* Didn't the secretary tell you that we're in a meeting right now? If you'll wait outside, I'll be able to see you in about an hour.
>
> *Martin:* In your next job, maybe you should train your secretary better. Anyway, I can't waste time sitting around in hallways. Everyone in this room knows why I'm here. You've got a choice, Jack. You can cooperate with me, or you can lose any credibility you still have in this company.
>
> *Davis:* If I didn't have any more experience than you do, I wouldn't be so quick to throw my weight around. But if you think you know it all already, I guess you won't need any help from me.
>
> *Martin:* What I know is that this department has gone downhill under your leadership, and it's my job to turn it around. You can go home right now, if you want—but if you're smart, you'll stay and help. The vice president wants my report on the transition. You'll be a lot better off if I can tell him you've been cooperative.

Moviegoers cheer when bullies get their comeuppance. It can be satisfying to give the verbal equivalent of a kick in the groin to someone who deserves it. In this exchange, Martin establishes that she is tough, even dangerous. But such coercive tactics can be expensive in the long run. She is likely to win this battle because her hand is stronger, but she may lose the war. She increases Davis's antagonism, and her attack may offend him and frighten her new staff. Even if they dislike Davis, they might see Martin as arrogant and callous. She lays the ground for a counterattack, and may have done political damage that will be difficult to reverse.

Sophisticated political leaders prefer to avoid naked demonstrations of power, looking instead for ways to appeal to the self-interest of potential adversaries:

Davis: Didn't the secretary tell you that we're in a meeting right now? If you'll wait outside, I'll be able to see you in about an hour.

Martin: (pleasantly) Jack, if it's OK with you, I'd prefer to skip the games and go to work. I expect this department to be a winner, and I hope that's what we all want. I also would like to manage the transition in a way that's good for your career, Jack, and for the careers of others in the room.

Davis: If I need advice from you on my career, I'll ask.

Martin: OK, but the vice president has asked me to let him know about the cooperation I get here. I'd like to be able to say that everyone has been helping me as much as possible. Is that what you'd like, too?

Davis: I've known the vice president a lot longer than you have. I can talk to him myself.

Martin: I know, Jack, he's told me that. In fact, I just came from his office. If you'd like, we could both go see him right now.

Davis: Uh, no, not right now.

Martin: Well, then, let's get on with it. Do you want to finish what you were discussing, or is this a good time for us to develop some agreement on how we're going to work together?

In this instance, Martin is direct and diplomatic. She uses a light touch in dismissing Davis's opening salvo. ("I'd prefer to skip the games.") She speaks directly to both Davis's interest in his career and her subordinates' interest in theirs. She deftly deflates his posturing by asking if he wants to go with her to talk to the vice president. Clearly, she is confident of her political position and knows that his bluster has little to back it up.

Note that in both political scenarios, Martin draws on her power resources. In the first, she uses those resources to humiliate Davis, but in the second, her approach is more subtle. She conserves her political capital and takes charge while leaving Davis with as much pride as possible, achieving something closer to a win-win than a win-lose outcome.

A Symbolic Scenario

Symbolic leaders believe that the most important part of a leader's job is inspiration—giving people something they can believe in. People become excited about and committed to a place with a unique culture, a special place where they feel that what they do is really making a difference. Effective symbolic leaders are passionate about making the organization unique in its niche and communicating that passion to others. They use dramatic symbols to excite people and to give them a sense of the organization's mission. They are visible and energetic. They create slogans, tell stories, hold rallies, give awards, appear where they are least expected, and manage by wandering around.

Symbolic leaders are sensitive to an organization's history and culture. They seek to use the best of an organization's traditions and values as a base for building a culture that has cohesiveness and meaning. They articulate a vision that communicates the organization's unique capabilities and mission.

At first glance, Olivia Martin's encounter with Jack Davis might seem a poor candidate for the symbolic approach outlined in this scenario. An ineffective effort could produce embarrassing results, making the would-be symbolic leader look foolish:

Davis: Didn't the secretary tell you that we're in a meeting right now? If you'll wait outside, I'll be able to see you in about an hour.

Martin: It's great to see that you're all hard at work. It's proof that we all share a commitment to excellence in customer service. In fact, I've already made up buttons for all the staff. Here—I have one for each of you. They read, "The customer is always first." They look great, and they communicate the spirit that we all want in the department. Go on with your meeting. I can use the hour to talk to some of the staff about their visions for the department. *(She walks out of the office.)*

Davis: *(to remaining staff)* Did you believe that? I told you they hired a real space cadet to replace me. Maybe you didn't believe me, but you just saw it with your own eyes.

Martin's symbolic direction might be on the right track, but symbols work only when they are attuned to the context and make sense to members of a group or organization. As a newcomer to the department culture, she needs to pay close attention to her audience. Meaningless symbols antagonize, and empty symbolic events backfire.

Conversely, a skillful symbolic leader understands that a situation of challenge and stress can serve as a powerful opportunity to articulate values and build a sense of mission. Martin does both, in a well-formed symbolic approach to Davis's gruffness:

Davis: Didn't the secretary tell you that we're in a meeting right now? If you'll wait outside, I'll be able to see you in about an hour.

Martin: (smiling) Maybe this is just the traditional hazing ritual in this department, Jack, but let me ask a question: If one of our customers came through the door right now, would you ask her to wait outside for an hour?

Davis: If she just came barging in like you did, sure.

Martin: Are you working on something that's more important than responding to our customers?

Davis: They're not your customers. You've only been here five minutes.

Martin: True, but I've been with this company long enough to know the importance of putting customers first.

Davis: Look, you don't know the first thing about how this department functions. Before you go off on some customer crusade, you ought to learn a little about how we do things.

Martin: There's a lot I can learn from all of you, and I'm eager to get started. For example, I'm very interested in your ideas on how we can make this a department where as soon as people walk in, they get the sense that this is a place where people care, are responsive, and genuinely want to be helpful. I'd like that to be true for anyone who comes in—a staff member, a customer, or just someone who got lost and came into the wrong office. That's not the message I got from my initiation a couple of minutes ago, but I'm sure we can think of lots of ways to change that. How does that fit with your image of what the department should be like?

Notice how Martin recasts the conversation. Instead of engaging in a personal confrontation with Davis, she focuses on the department's core values. She brings her "customer first" commitment with her, but she avoids positioning that value as something imposed from outside. Instead, she grounds it in an experience everyone in the room has just shared: the way she was greeted when she entered. Like many successful symbolic leaders, she is attuned to the cues about values and culture that are expressed in everyday life. She communicates her philosophy, but she also asks questions to draw out Davis and her new staff members. If she can use the organization's history to advantage in rekindling a commitment to customer service, she is off to a good start.

BENEFITS AND RISKS OF REFRAMING

The multiple replays of the Davis-Martin incident illustrate both the power and the risks of reframing. The frames are powerful because of their ability to spur imagination and generate new insights and options. But each frame has limits as well as strengths, and each can be applied well or poorly.

Frames can be used as scripts, or scenarios, to guide action in high-stakes circumstances. By changing your script, you can change how you appear, what you do, and how your audience sees you. You can create the possibility of transforming everyday situations. Few of us have the dramatic skill and versatility of a professional actor, but you can alter what you do by choosing an alternative script or scenario. You have been learning how to do this since birth. Both men and women, for example, typically employ different scenarios for same-sex and opposite-sex encounters. Students who are guarded and formal when talking to a professor become energized and intimate when talking to friends. Managers who are polite and deferential with the boss may be gruff and autocratic with subordinates and then come home at night to romp playfully with their kids. The tenderhearted neighbor becomes a ruthless competitor when his company's market share is threatened. The tough-minded drill instructor who terrorizes new recruits bows to authority when faced by a colonel.

Consciously or not, we all read situations to figure out what scene we're in and what role we've been assigned, so that we can respond in character. But it's important to ask ourselves whether the drama is the one we want and to recognize that we have latitude as to which character to play and how to interpret the script. In adapting to cues of the theatrical moment, we don't want to compromise our own sense of identity. But we have editorial license to alter the scene and recast the drama.

The essence of reframing is examining the same situation from multiple vantage points. The effective leader changes lenses when things don't make sense or aren't working. Reframing offers the promise of powerful new options, even though it cannot guarantee that every new strategy will be successful. Each lens offers distinctive advantages, but each has its blind spots and shortcomings.

The structural frame risks ignoring everything that falls outside the rational scope of tasks, procedures, policies, and organization charts. Structural thinking can overestimate the power of authority and underestimate the authority of power. Paradoxically, overreliance on structural assumptions and a narrow emphasis on rationality can lead to an irrational neglect of human, political, and cultural variables crucial to effective action.

Adherents of the human resource frame sometimes cling to a romanticized view of human nature in which everyone hungers for growth and collaboration. Human resource enthusiasts can be overly optimistic about integrating individual and organizational needs while neglecting structure and the stubborn realities of conflict and scarcity.

The political frame captures dynamics that other frames miss, but has its own limits. A fixation on politics easily becomes a cynical self-fulfilling prophecy, reinforcing conflict and mistrust while sacrificing opportunities for rational discourse, collaboration, and hope. Political action is too often interpreted as amoral scheming.

The symbolic frame offers powerful insight into fundamental issues of meaning and belief, as well as possibilities for shaping people into a cohesive group with a shared mission. But its concepts are also elusive; effectiveness depends on the artistry of the user. Symbols are sometimes seen as mere fluff or camouflage, the tools of a charlatan who seeks to manipulate the unsuspecting or an awkward attempt that embarrasses more than energizes people at work.

REFRAMING FOR NEWCOMERS AND OUTSIDERS

Martin's initial encounter with Davis exemplifies many of the challenges and tests that leaders confront as they move forward in their careers. The different scenarios offer a glimmer of what they might run into, depending on how they size up a situation. Managers feel powerless and trapped when they rely on only one or two frames. This is particularly true for those who are less powerful, which may include newcomers and underdogs—women, minorities, and members of other groups who experience "the dogged frustration of people living daily in a system not made for them and with no plans soon to adjust for them or their differences."[1] These outsiders are less likely to get a second or third chance when they fail.

Although progressive organizations have made heroic strides in building fairer opportunity structures, the path to success is still fraught with obstacles for the less powerful. Judicious reframing can help them transform managerial traps into promising leadership opportunities. And the more often individuals break through the glass ceiling or out of the corporate ghetto, the more quickly those barriers will disappear altogether.

CONCLUSION

Leaders can harness frames as scenarios, or scripts, to generate unique approaches to challenging circumstances. In planning for a high-stakes meeting or a tense encounter, they can imagine and experiment with novel ways to play their roles. Until reframing becomes instinctive, it takes more than the few seconds that Olivia Martin had to generate an effective response in every lens. In practicing any new skill—playing tennis, flying an airplane, or handling a tough leadership challenge—the process is often slow and painstaking at first. But as skill improves, it gets easier, faster, and more fluid, and the role of a leader becomes less vexing and more rewarding.

Images of Leadership
Can Crooked Kites Fly?

I deally we would all be versatile leaders who see the world through multiple lenses. In reality, most of us have a narrower field of vision. We prefer some ways of interpreting reality and neglect others. If our preferences were measured and plotted on a four-dimensional grid, we'd look lopsided. The shape of our leadership "kite," depicting our cognitive leanings, can position us for success—or disaster. It all depends on how well we can adapt our mental images to align with the challenges we face.

You don't have to be equally comfortable with all four frames. If certain areas fall outside your comfort zone, expand your field of vision— or work with someone who can help cover for your blind spots. That approach paid off for Facebook founder Mark Zuckerberg. The shy and geeky Zuckerberg is strong on ideas and technology but weak on executive presence. He was wise enough to complement himself with his chief operating officer, Google veteran Sheryl Sandberg. She brought a Harvard MBA, interpersonal skills, and a steady, adult hand to a company known for its chaotic, frat house atmosphere. "The dynamic on the management team," Zuckerberg commented, "has improved a huge amount since she joined."[1] Sandberg focuses on management, public relations, and marketing, leaving Zuckerberg free to indulge his passion for the Facebook website. "Sandberg's hefty portfolio and her fluid, trusting relationship with Zuckerberg are liberating for him. She does all the things he doesn't want to do so he can focus on what he likes."[2]

Every pattern has virtues and shortcomings, and works better in some situations than in others. In this chapter, we look at prominent business leaders who have made their crooked kites fly. As you study their examples, reflect on how well your preferences serve you now and will continue to serve going forward. (If you have not already done so, use the Leadership Orientations survey in the Appendix to assess the shape of your own leadership kite by completing the survey, plotting your scores on the figure, and connecting the dots. An online version of the instrument is available at http://www.josseybassbusiness.com/2013/07/assessment-leadership-orientations-self-assessment.html.)

METRICS MAESTRO: AMAZON'S JEFF BEZOS

In 2005, with Amazon's profits and stock price sinking, a business journalist wrote that it was time for Jeff Bezos, Amazon's founder and longtime chief executive, to turn over the reins to a professional manager with deep operations experience.[3] The writer pegged Amazon as a retailer gone adrift that needed someone to jack up profit margins. Bezos, who had much bigger plans for Amazon, ignored the advice and kept after his goal of expanding his company into the largest Internet purveyor of almost everything, including e-readers and web services. Seven years later, in 2012, Forbes rated Bezos the best CEO in America: "the corporate chief that others most want to meet, emulate and deify."[4] A brilliant strategist, demanding leader, and one of the smartest guys in any room, Bezos is a contemporary example of a leader whose strong structural orientation is central to his success. Figure 11.1 shows our estimate of Bezos's frames configuration.

The structural frame dominates, closely followed by a strong symbolic orientation. The combination is captured in a phrase Bezos uses to describe Amazon: "a culture of metrics."[5] Bezos has also shown political savvy in navigating Amazon's many external battles with competitors and content creators (such as publishers and authors). At the heart of Bezos's approach to leadership is a relentless focus on the customer: "Amazon tracks its performance against about 500 measurable goals. Nearly 80% relate to customer objectives. Some Amazonians try to reduce out-of-stock merchandise. Others race to build a bigger library of downloadable movies. Intricate algorithms turn one group of shoppers' past habits into custom

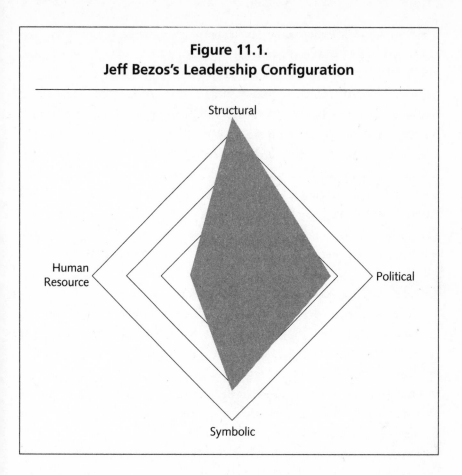

Figure 11.1.
Jeff Bezos's Leadership Configuration

recommendations for new customers. Hourly best seller lists identify what's hot. Weekly reviews keep track of who is on course—and where corrective attention is needed."[6]

Bezos's focus is crystal clear: the best possible customer service at the lowest possible cost. He pays little attention to the human resource proposition: "if you take care of your people, they'll take care of your customers." He flattens subordinates with comments like, "Are you lazy or just incompetent?" or "This document was clearly written by the B team. Can someone get me the A team document?"[7] Bezos believes in "coddling his 164 million customers, not his 56,000 employees."[8]

He is obsessive about minimizing costs that don't benefit consumers. That's why Amazon executives fly coach and work at cheap, particleboard desks. At one distribution center, as an alternative to the cost of air conditioning, Amazon had paramedics on standby during heat waves to aid employees overcome by heat. Amazon's tough approach produced various forms of employee resistance, including theft, unionization efforts, and one creative worker's own do-it-yourself job enrichment program. He created a little cave for himself in an obscure corner of a distribution center, furnishing it with items borrowed from Amazon's shelves. He punched in each morning, spent the day relaxing in his refuge, and punched out at night. His career was brief.

Bezos's salary, less than $100,000, hasn't budged since 1998 (though his Amazon stock has made him rich; *Forbes* estimated his wealth at $27 billion in late 2013). But he is a risk taker who will spend big to build the business. He invested heavily in Kindle for years before it finally became a viable product. More recently, he announced a plan to use midget drones to fly packages directly to the customer's door.

Amazon's success depends on making it as quick and easy as possible for customers to find what they're looking for and get it delivered promptly to their home or office. This means that the website (where customers browse and buy) and the distribution centers (that turn digital orders into physical shipments) must be tightly aligned. Bezos and Amazon continually obsess over making sure systems perform.

Bezos is a hands-on leader who reads customer emails to stay in touch with what's working and what isn't. He tracks the metrics, pays close attention to operational specifics, relentlessly attacks waste, sets demanding targets, and is vigilant about ensuring accountability. Amazon has discovered, for example, that even a 0.1-second delay in rendering a web page can produce a 1 percent drop in customer activity, so Bezos pushes for constant effort to make the site faster and more responsive.

Amazon's many metrics and huge database on customer behavior are a treasure trove for continuous improvement. Efforts to give you precisely what you're looking for and to get it to you on time are relentless. In 2011, Bezos was proud that Amazon kept its promise to deliver goods to meet the Christmas deadline 99.99 percent of the time, but this still meant that they missed once in every ten thousand shipments. He wanted to get that number to 100 percent, and was not happy when many Christmas gifts missed the holiday because delivery partners such as UPS couldn't keep up with the holiday demand in 2013.

Jeff Bezos's leadership formula combines a strong emphasis on structure and technology with a demanding, customer-centric culture. One reason it works is that Amazon customers transact business with a website, not people. Amazon customers have learned not to expect friendly sales clerks who offer a cheerful greeting or in-depth product knowledge. Instead, customers reach a site that makes it easy to find preferred or panned needles in haystacks. The result is a business that consistently ranks in the top ten for customer service among online retailers. There are other ways to achieve success in online retailing, however. Surprisingly, one of the clearest contrasting examples is Zappos, a business that Amazon bought for roughly a billion dollars in 2009.

LEADER OF THE TRIBE: ZAPPOS'S TONY HSIEH

Zappos began when a frustrated shoe buyer, Nick Swinmurn, couldn't find what he wanted in local stores or online. He decided to launch a website, shoesite.com, that he soon renamed Zappos.[9] Needing capital, he approached Tony Hsieh and Alfred Lin, who headed a small investment firm with the playful name Venture Frogs. Hsieh and Lin eventually pumped in more than $10 million.[10] Hsieh came on board as co-CEO and then took over when Swinmurn moved up to board chair. Hsieh had plenty of room to practice his unorthodox brand of leadership, centered on a few key ideas. Figure 11.2 shows our estimate of Hsieh's frames configuration.

Delivering Happiness is the title of Hsieh's book about Zappos. Inspired in part by a customer who wrote that Zappos delivers happiness in a box, Hsieh is passionate about his conviction that if an organization delivers happiness to employees, they'll do the same for customers, whose loyalty will make the business successful.

"Fun" and "weird" are two of the words most often used to describe what it's like to work at Zappos. The company isn't unique in offering its people free food and snacks, computers in an Internet café, or frequent parties. But it's one of the few where singing, dancing, and costume parades are commonplace. Or where employee creativity shines in dozens of online videos about life at Zappos. These include a Zappos Family Musical[11] and a clip showing a Zappos employee celebrating happy hour by slapping the CEO on his face.

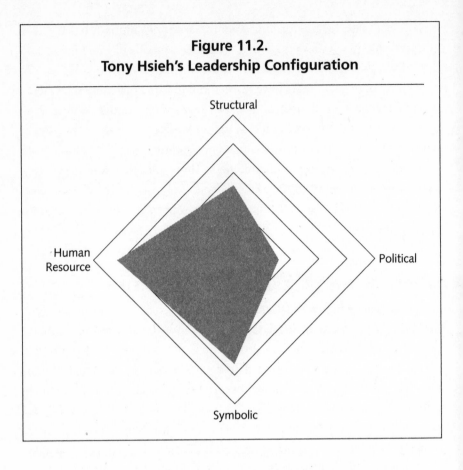

Figure 11.2.
Tony Hsieh's Leadership Configuration

Structural

Human
Resource

Political

Symbolic

Hsieh describes Zappos's culture as the company's number-one priority, and adds, "Our belief is that if you get the culture right, then most of the other stuff—like great customer service or building a long lasting, enduring brand—will happen naturally."[12] Zappos has anchored its culture in a set of core values that include "Deliver WOW Through Service," "Embrace and Drive Change," "Create Fun and a Little Weirdness," "Be Adventurous, Creative, and Open-Minded," and "Pursue Growth and Learning."

Before Hsieh joined Zappos, he cofounded a successful Internet firm, Linkexchange.com, but eventually decided to sell the business (to Microsoft in 1998 for $265 million) because he no longer enjoyed coming to work. The fatal error, he believed, had been hiring for skill rather than cultural fit. Hsieh didn't want to make that mistake again, and every Zappos job applicant is interviewed for alignment with the company's core values. After they've been through initial training, Zappos offers new employees $2,000 to quit. Few accept, but it's a powerful test of commitment and a way to weed out people who aren't right for the culture.

All new employees, regardless of position, go through a training program that includes a week at the Zappos distribution center in Kentucky, and a tour at the call center talking to customers. Most of Zappos's business comes from the website rather than the phone, but the call center gives new employees a way to get to know the customers and Zappos's customer service values. Unlike most call center workers, Zappos employees don't use scripts and aren't measured on efficient use of time. Instead, their job is to do what it takes to make customers happy. If it takes an hour or two to solve a customer's problem, or if they have to go to a competitor's website to find what a customer wants, that's what's expected.

Creativity, fun, and weirdness intermingle to give customers more than they expect. Zappos customers often use the word "love" to describe their feelings about the site, raving about the selection, service, return policy, and free shipping in both directions. That pays off in loyal customers who keep coming back.

AUTHENTIC ENGINEER: XEROX'S URSULA BURNS

After twenty years of climbing the ladder at Xerox, Ursula Burns was ready to quit. She didn't see much future in a company with a mountain of debt, no cash, and a corrosive culture of executive infighting. The stock price had fallen from $64 to $7 a share, and a CEO recruited from IBM had been fired after serving less than a year. Still, colleagues and board members told Burns that Xerox needed her, and the new CEO, Anne Mulcahy (profiled in Chapter Six) convinced her that she could help save the company.

Mulcahy and Burns were both Xerox lifers who had known each other for years, but they had come up through different paths: Mulcahy via sales, Burns through engineering and operations. One of the first assignments Burns took on for Mulcahy was to persuade unions that Xerox had to outsource many of its manufacturing jobs to survive. It was a tough sell, but Burns used her basic approach to leadership: "One of the things I've learned is that if you can know your facts, and you build up your opinions with some facts and data, as well as some emotional conviction, you can generally get people to listen to the general story and direction."[13]

The unions bought her argument that fewer jobs were better than no jobs. When Mulcahy retired as CEO in 2009, she and the board agreed that Ursula Burns should take over the job. Burns's promotion generated a rash of media attention because of two firsts: Burns was the first African American woman to head a Fortune 500 company and the first woman to succeed another woman as CEO of a major U.S. business. Figure 11.3 illustrates Burns's leadership configuration.

Burns's leadership configuration shows strengths across all four frames, but she is highest on structure and human resource, lowest on the political frame. The pattern reflects her background as an engineer who worked her way up to head worldwide manufacturing for Xerox. Her structural leanings were evident in her willingness "to do whatever it takes—dismantle the company's manufacturing unit that shaped her career; cut back or

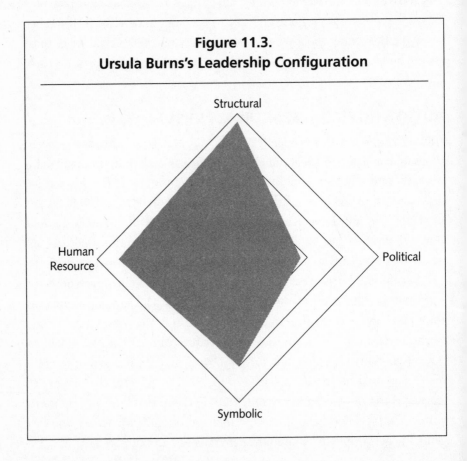

Figure 11.3.
Ursula Burns's Leadership Configuration

Structural

Human Resource

Political

Symbolic

eliminate products that once defined the Xerox brand; branch out into uncertain (and risky) new areas of business—in an effort to reposition the company in an era of technological upheaval."[14]

Her signature initiative was persuading Lynn Blodgett, the CEO of Affiliated Computer Services (ACS), that merging with Xerox would be a win-win for both companies. Burns saw ACS, a $6 billion supplier of back-office services, as the perfect partner to accelerate a shift in the Xerox business mix toward less emphasis on hardware and more on services. ACS had multiple suitors, but Burns helped seal the deal by sending Blodgett on a tour of Xerox's European research center in France. For a data guy like ACS's Blodgett, it was love at first sight. "I was already happy with our technology," he says. "But this was going to make an immediate difference to us."[15]

Once the ACS merger was in place, Burns deployed her people skills—a combination of hugs and straight talk—in a campaign to convince Xerox managers that the company's success required less "terminal niceness" and a lot more candor. In effect, she was hoping to convince her colleagues to be more like her. Burns's style had always been to tell it like she saw it. She was known for her directness rather than her tact, which sometimes annoyed her bosses but had helped her career.

Burns saw her leadership approach as more about people than politics. Women, she felt, had "been taught to nurture and work in groups. You've been handed something to take care of—here's a baby, here's someone to dress—there is this natural ability to include more than compete. Now, there's always competition. I definitely compete, but the role of competition can be too absolute—winning at any cost. It's just not there for me. More of a balance is there for me."[16] Early in her career, Burns's talent compensated for her lack of political savvy, but mentors helped her polish the rough edges, improve her listening skills, and develop the political skills to move up in a very competitive environment.

WARRIOR ARTIST: APPLE'S STEVE JOBS

There was never any doubt about Steve Jobs's genius, and if you look at his profile, there's very little doubt that he saw organizations as political contests. In 1985, he found himself locked in a battle with just about every senior manager at Apple, a company he had cofounded with Steve Wozniak nine years earlier. Apple's marketing chief slammed Jobs for "management by character assassination."[17] John Sculley, the CEO whom Jobs had lured away from PepsiCo, reluctantly confronted his former patron for "bad-mouthing him as a bozo behind his back."[18] After Sculley learned that Jobs was planning a coup to push him out, he and the board agreed that Jobs had to go.

Being sacked took the wind from Jobs's sails for a time. "It was awful-tasting medicine but I guess the patient needed it."[19] After his bruised ego healed, he went on to invest $50 million in a small computer graphics unit that evolved into Pixar. There, lessons learned at Apple and his failed startup, NeXT, served him well. Jobs understood more clearly that the way to build great products is to build a cohesive organization, and his way of treating people had softened somewhat.

In 1997, Jobs returned to rescue Apple from a death spiral. He was much like the leader fired from Apple twelve years earlier: demanding and charismatic, charming and infuriating, erratic and focused, opinionated and receptive. The difference was in how he thought and how he led. In short order after he returned, he radically simplified Apple's product line, built a loyal and talented leadership team, and turned his old company into a hit-making machine as reliable as Pixar. Jobs's leadership configuration is shown in Figure 11.4.

Jobs was a master of the symbolic frame. The public knew him as a charismatic salesman whose flair for drama could transform product announcements into compelling theater that captivated the media and the public. He was also a design maven who would settle for nothing less than one "insanely great" product after another. Those who worked with him talked about "Steve's reality distortion field" and "the world according to Steve," reflecting his flair for framing any project or product as an opportunity to "put a dent in the universe." In introducing new Apple products, he transformed digital boxes into mystical wonders conjured by a magical wizard. In advance of a launch, he stoked the fire of expectations and cultivated the media. In the run-up to the launch of the iPhone in 2007, Jobs called the editor in chief at *Time*, telling him that Apple was about to announce the greatest thing it had ever done. He added that he wanted to give *Time* an exclusive, but that no one at *Time* was smart enough to write

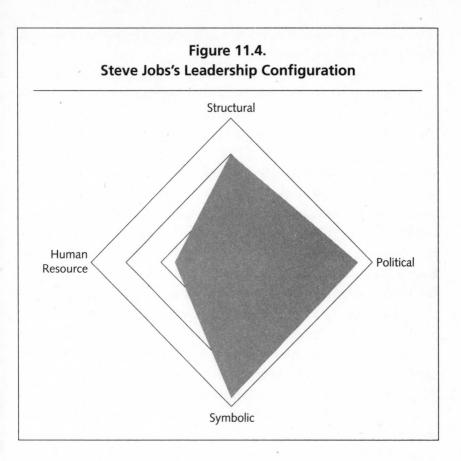

Figure 11.4.
Steve Jobs's Leadership Configuration

the article. *Time* scrambled to find a writer smart enough for Steve, and Jobs got the publicity he wanted.

At the launch itself, Jobs connected to Apple's history by inviting Steve Wozniak and the heroes who had developed the first Mac.[20] He opened by telling the faithful, "Every once in a while a revolutionary product comes along that changes everything," offering the Macintosh and the iPod as examples. Then he built to his climax. "Today, we're introducing three revolutionary products of this class. The first one is a widescreen iPod with touch controls." The audience applauded. "The second is a revolutionary mobile phone." The applause grew louder. "And the third is a breakthrough Internet communications device." Still more applause. He repeated the list three times, revving up his audience for the punch line. "Are you getting it? These are not three separate devices. This is one device, and we are calling it the iPhone. Today, Apple is reinventing the phone."[21] The audience laughed, cried, and cheered wildly.

Beyond the showman, Jobs was also a lifelong warrior, as we saw in his battle with Disney chief Michael Eisner (described in Chapter Seven). Short-tempered but supremely confident in his own intuition and opinions, Jobs regularly went to war with anyone who got in his way. Even though he was a rebel all his life, he also had an appreciation for organizational design. He built a distinctive structure at Apple that reflected his own personality and biases. He and his small executive team were the nerve center of a highly centralized, functional organization.[22] Everything important was hammered out in that group's Monday morning meetings. As Jobs described it, "We look at every single product under development. I put out an agenda. Eighty percent is the same as it was the last week, and we just walk down it every single week. We don't have a lot of process at Apple, but that's one of the few things we do just to all stay on the same page."[23] A unified team at the top could turn on a dime to exploit new opportunities or to correct error, and its job was more manageable because of Jobs's insistence on doing only a few great things rather than trying to do everything. "Jobs often contrasts Apple's approach with its competitors'. Sony, he has said, had too many divisions to create the iPod."[24]

Like Jeff Bezos, Jobs rarely displayed the warmth and sensitivity that are often associated with human resource leadership. He cared little about other people's feelings and was famously tyrannical and punitive. An example was a meeting he called for the team that had developed MobileMe, a software application that had failed to deliver on its promises. After asking the team to explain what MobileMe was supposed to do, he responded, "So why the fuck doesn't it do that?" He excoriated them for tarnishing Apple's reputation and told them they should all hate each other.[25] People feared his temper, but admired his genius and craved his approval. He divided the world into "A players" and bozos. If he decided you were a bozo, your career at Apple was likely to end soon, but he knew he needed great people to produce great products, and loved working with people he respected, including Apple's brilliant design chief, Jony Ive, and Jobs's eventual successor as CEO, Tim Cook.

CONCLUSION

Versatility in understanding and applying all four frames is valuable for any leader, but few of us are completely symmetrical. Understanding your current strengths and weaknesses is a starting point for becoming a more balanced leader. Equally important is to recognize the degree of alignment between your configuration and the leadership challenges you face. Jeff Bezos, for example, has made Amazon successful with a business model that compensates for his disinterest in human resource issues by relying on metrics and technology. By contrast, Tony Hsieh has used his passion for people and culture to build Zappos into a customer service phenomenon. It is vital to know how well your leadership kite positions you to take on your most significant opportunities and challenges. The endless parade of leaders—like Ron Johnson in Chapter One—who crash into a wall they didn't see is destructive to all involved. If you recognize your blind spots, you can work on expanding your vision or collaborating with others who complement your worldview because they are attuned to things that you might miss.

Leadership and Change

Machiavelli observed many years ago, "It must be realized that there is nothing more difficult to plan, more uncertain of success, or more dangerous to manage than the establishment of a new order of [things]; for he who introduces [change] makes enemies of all those who derived advantage from the old order and finds but lukewarm defenders among those who stand to gain from the new one."[1]

His observation helps explain the durable truth in the adage, "the more things change, the more they stay the same." Many leaders have learned the hard way that departing from the status quo is risky business. You might be a veteran of the change wars, still licking your wounds, or an eager aspirant waiting for your turn. In this chapter, we examine what makes change so difficult, first by exploring the limits of leadership. We then contrast leaders who impose change on an organization with those who stimulate the latent energy for improvement that is already present. Next, we use the four frames to identify barriers to innovation and to anticipate what leaders can do to move change forward. Finally, we examine the remarkable turnaround that Alan Mulally engineered in bringing Ford Motor Company back to life.

LIMITS OF LEADERSHIP

We most often portray leaders as change agents—carriers of innovation and transformation. In politics, for example, new candidates running for office blame the incumbents for anything that's gone wrong, while promising a better future. In 2008, Barack Obama promised "New Hope," but fulfilling that pledge was daunting in the face of the recession he inherited from his predecessor. By 2012, Obama was the incumbent, and his Republican opponent, Mitt Romney, promised to "restore America's greatness" by fixing everything Obama had broken. One election after another, voters are asked to put hope above experience and to believe the message, "I can do what the incumbent didn't do."

This takes us to a perennial question about leadership: Do the times make leaders, or do leaders make the times? The prevailing view is that leaders can and should make a difference. However, there is much merit in the opposing, more disturbing view that circumstances often overwhelm leaders. Cohen and March provocatively compare the command-and-control capabilities of college presidents to the situation facing the driver of a skidding automobile: "The marginal judgments he makes, his skill, and his luck will probably make some difference to the life prospects of his riders. As a result, his responsibilities are heavy. But whether he is convicted of manslaughter or receives a medal for heroism is largely outside his control."[2] The same assertion holds for leaders in almost any organization.

The backing and faith of followers are vital to leaders' ability to bring about successful change. When people believe in you, they will give you credit when good things happen and are less likely to blame you when things go wrong. "Successful leadership is having followers who believe in the power of the leader. By believing, people are encouraged to link positive events with leadership behavior."[3] Leaders can make a difference in moving an organization forward, but they are wise to undertake change with a dose of humility. Attempting to command an organization to perform differently is usually futile. Command is about authority, control, and dominion—which most leaders learn are in short supply. But leaders do have influence, which *Webster's* dictionary defines as "the power of persons or things to affect others, seen only in its effects." The difference between command and influence can be seen in comparing two different leader roles: carrier or catalyst of change.

CARRIERS VERSUS CATALYSTS OF CHANGE

Leaders often undertake change in one of two different ways. The first is to impose an innovation imported from outside, particularly one currently in vogue. The second approach is to stimulate or inspire energy in an organization by drawing on historical memory, a flicker of cultural readiness, and a reservoir of employee initiative.

The first mind-set is exemplified in the wide diffusion of Six Sigma, which began as a statistical concept but evolved into a range of metrics, methods, and management techniques intended to reduce defects and increase quality in products and services. First developed at Motorola in 1986, it was later honed by Jack Welch at General Electric. Six Sigma became an integral part of the GE Way. It flowered as a new corporate shibboleth in the 1990s after its success at GE.

When Welch retired, several potential successors who lost out to Jeff Immelt for the top job at GE left the company for new CEO positions, taking the Six Sigma techniques with them. One was James McNerney, who was snapped up by 3M in 2001 to bring some discipline to a legendary enterprise that seemed to be losing its edge. Profit and sales growth were erratic, and the stock price had languished.

McNerney wasted no time. Thousands of 3M workers trained to earn the Six Sigma title of "Black Belt." These converts pioneered company-wide Six Sigma initiatives, such as boosting the tempo of production by reducing variation and eliminating pointless steps in manufacturing. The Black Belt elite maintained metrics that tracked both overall and "neighborhood" efforts to systematize and streamline all aspects of work—including R&D.

In the short run, McNerney's strategy paid off. Indicators of productivity improved, costs were trimmed, and the stock price soared. But Six Sigma's standardization began to intrude on 3M's historical emphasis on innovation. Prior to McNerney's arrival, new ideas were accorded almost unlimited time and funding to germinate—with little accountability. This approach had given birth to legendary products such as Scotch Tape and Post-it Notes. No more. The new-idea spigot began to dry up.

McNerney left 3M in 2005 to become the new CEO of Boeing. Art Fry (inventor of Post-it Notes) lamented, "What's remarkable is how fast a culture can be torn apart. [McNerney] didn't kill it because he wasn't here long enough. But if he had been here much longer, I think he would have."[4] McNerney's successor, George Buckley, observed in retrospect, "Perhaps one of the mistakes that we made as a company—it's one of the dangers of Six Sigma—is that when you value sameness more than you value creativity, I think you potentially undermine the heart and soul of a company like 3M."[5]

Other former GE executives, such as Robert Nardelli, who was credited with undermining employee morale and customer service at Home Depot (his story was told in Chapter One), had similar experiences. Importing an innovation from one organization to another is risky business. It's akin to bringing a plant from one ecosystem to another. It might succeed, but the import may die quickly (like palm trees in Siberia) or become a destructive pest (like kudzu in the United States and elsewhere). Leaders as imposers of change are often headed for trouble because their initiative is seen as something alien that needs to be snuffed out.

More promising are change efforts that are rooted in an organization's history, culture, and people and built on a shared understanding of the current challenges. We have seen examples in earlier chapters, including Anne Mulcahy at Xerox, Howard Schultz at Starbucks, and Lou Gerstner at IBM.

In 2007, Microsoft took a similar path in an effort to solve a problem that perplexed CEO Steve Ballmer. Microsoft's stock was slipping, products were delayed, and observers inside and outside perceived the company as "flabby, middle-aged and un-hip"—especially in contrast to Google.[6] Ballmer could have brought in a fix-it expert, such as a new human resource chief, to implement a company-driven antidote to the malaise. Instead, Ballmer reached down into the ranks and promoted a maverick to rekindle the company's spirit. He elevated Lisa Brummel, a product manager beloved for her unconventional ways and dress, to the role of chief people officer.

One of Brummel's first initiatives might seem strange to structural thinkers: she brought back the towels that had been a feature of employee locker rooms until removed earlier to cut costs. The lost towels had become a heated subject in internal blogs, primarily as symbols of how little the company cared. Beyond helping with Seattle's chronic drizzle, the towels were a small but treasured perk of working at Microsoft. Brummel also replaced the self-service "industrial sludge" coffeemakers with Starbucks machines that fit better with Seattle's barista ethos.

The next target for Brummel's magic wand was Microsoft's dreaded performance review procedure. Devised by Ballmer himself, the ranking system was a zero-sum game in which employees competed for their individual shares of a limited purse. Managers could give only so many A's, even if several employees had performed exceptionally well. It was a touchy issue pitting Brummel against Ballmer, but she won and implemented a system that gave managers more discretion and tied raises and bonuses to a combination of pay grade and annual performance.

Brummel opened up communication by moving the internal "underground" blog into the public spotlight. She changed the company's office décor from institutional drab to modern chic and created a mobile medicine service to dispatch company physicians to employees' homes for emergencies. Brummel's initiatives raised morale, cut attrition, and, in many instances, one-upped Google. Brummel developed initiatives from the ground up as internal catalysts for change, rather than relying on programs imported from somewhere else. Instead of taking things away or imposing things no one wanted, she gave people innovations they welcomed. Among the outcomes of these efforts was recognition at the top of a ranking of best multinational workplaces for 2011.[7]

The point is not that practices never transfer well from one organization to another. Six Sigma, for example, has worked well in many different companies. But if leaders hope to bring an idea or process from one organization to another, they need to think carefully and comprehensively about similarities and differences in the structure, people, politics, and culture of the two organizations. They also need to ask if an organic, home-grown innovation might have a much better chance of success than one imported from somewhere else.

THE FRAMES AND CHANGE

You're better off seeing quicksand before you're mired in it. Likewise, your chances of success are enhanced when you use the frames to help you see pitfalls and roadblocks in the road ahead. It rarely works to retrain people without revising roles or to revamp roles without retraining. Planning without broad-based participation that gives voice to political opposition is likely to provoke stiff resistance. Change alters power relationships and undermines existing agreements and pacts. Even more profoundly, it intrudes on deeply rooted symbolic forms, traditional ways, and rituals.

Whenever you or your organization contemplates significant revisions of the status quo, Exhibit 12.1 can serve as a helpful guide to what lies ahead. From a human resource perspective, the leader's role is to serve as a coach. Changes in routine and protocol undermine people's ability to perform with confidence and success. They feel puzzled, anxious, and insecure and need support and training to cope with new ways. Otherwise they may perform badly because they lack the understanding or skill they need to implement the new approach. They may resist or even sabotage the process because the changes don't make sense to them. Or, worse, they may comply superficially while covertly dragging their feet. Good coaches know the benefits of involvement, training, and support in building a winning team.

Exhibit 12.1.
Change: Barriers, Leader Roles, and Strategy

Frame	Barrier	Leader's Role	Strategy
Human Resource	Anxiety, incompetence	Coach	Training, support
Structural	Confusion, loss of direction	Architect	Redesign, restructure
Political	Conflict, opposing coalitions	Politician, peacemaker	Create arenas, manage conflict
Symbolic	Loss of meaning, clinging to past	Healer, storyteller	Ceremonies and rituals for letting go

The chart also suggests that support and training alone will not ensure success unless existing roles and relationships are realigned or reengineered to fit the new initiative. When things start to shift, people become unsure of what their duties are, how to relate to others, and who is in charge of what. Clarity, predictability, and rationality give way to confusion, loss of control, and a widespread sense that politics trumps policy. To minimize such difficulties, the leader as architect or engineer needs to redesign the social architecture of existing roles and relationships among people.

The chart also tells us that attempting an alteration to the status quo is a thorny political undertaking. As changes emerge, camps of supporters, opponents, and fence-sitters form quickly. Conflict, often avoided or smoothed over, explodes in divisive battles. Political infighting frequently undercuts authority and rationality. Leaders help by bringing submerged conflict to the surface and engaging it in open public arenas. Arenas are places or events that bring parties together to air issues and forge shared agreements. Through bargaining, compromises can be hammered out between outmoded ways and innovative ideals. The leader's role as politician and peacemaker is essential in dealing with the political turbulence and conflict that accompany significant change.

Finally, change produces feelings of loss because it severs ties to symbols that create meaning. When a relative or close friend dies, we suffer a gnawing sense of loss. We harbor similar feelings when a computer replaces old procedures, a logo changes after a merger, or a new leader replaces an old one. When these transitions take place in the workplace rather than in a family, feelings of loss are often denied, submerged, or attributed to other causes. Change typically triggers two conflicting symbolic responses. The first is to keep things as they were, to replay the past. The second is to ignore the loss and plunge into the future. Individuals or groups can get stuck in either form of denial, or they can bog down vacillating between the two.

In our personal lives, the pathway from loss to healing is culturally prescribed. Every culture outlines a bereavement process. In many societies, the sequence of ritual steps involves a wake, a funeral, a period of mourning, and some form of commemoration or celebration at the end. From a symbolic perspective, ritual is an essential companion to significant change. The leader helps by serving as a historian, storyteller, and healer.

We can see all these change dynamics at play in a case that depicts how a new leader used all four leadership lenses to transform an ailing company.

RESURRECTION AT FORD MOTOR

As Ford Motor Company was chalking up a $13 billion loss in 2006, chairman William Ford III reluctantly concluded that, hard as he had tried, he was failing in his efforts to save the company his great-grandfather had founded. He went in search of a seasoned leader smart enough to figure out where Ford needed to go, and tough enough to take on the infighting and entrenched mind-sets among executives and divisions that had defeated Bill Ford's best efforts. Eventually, he set his sights on Alan Mulally, the number-two executive at Boeing. Mulally, raised in Kansas and trained as an engineer, had earned a reputation during his long career in aviation as a strong leader who could put a troubled business on the right track. He loved Boeing and hated to leave, but Boeing's board had passed him over when it chose to bring in an outsider (James McNerney, who had received mixed reviews during his tenure as CEO at 3M) as CEO. Ford was eager to give him what Boeing wouldn't, and Mulally finally accepted an offer too good to refuse.

Before taking the job, Mulally did his homework and realized that he faced an almost impossible mission. To save the company, he needed to invest billions of dollars to improve Ford's lackluster product line. But Ford was burning cash and expected to lose $17 billion in the next year, so the path forward had to include layoffs, borrowing money, and cutting a new deal with the union. He faced daunting challenges from the view of all four frames, but surprised skeptics by hitting a high percentage of the pitches thrown his way.

To begin with, formidable political dynamics required immediate attention. Mulally recognized the need to get off on the right foot with the many constituencies that could make or break the needed changes. First up was the media, who would give the public its first impression of the new Ford chief. Step one in the media strategy was deliberate "leaks" of memos from Bill Ford in which he bemoaned the lack of honesty at the top of the company and called for fundamental change. Then Mulally and Ford's media relations staff cultivated key media contacts in advance and carefully staged the public announcement to ensure that the show opened to mostly rave reviews.

A second key constituency was the tens of thousands of Ford employees. On his second day at work, Mulally and Bill Ford led a joint town hall meeting in Detroit that was broadcast to workers around the world. After Ford introduced him, Mulally said he was honored to be asked to lead such a storied organization, then opened the floor to questions and gave upbeat but honest answers. Would he bring in a new executive team? No, he said, his team was right there. When the head of a strategic planning group asked if her unit would have a bigger role, he told her what she didn't want to hear: that strategy is a job for "our team," not a staff group.

Two weeks later, Mulally sent an email message to everyone at Ford that described his "first impressions." He was up front about some bad news: Ford's "gut-wrenching" circumstances meant that "some very good and loyal people are going to leave this company" in the months to come. But, he added, he was excited about the many people who were "bursting with ideas" and wanted to share them in emails, hallways, or the cafeteria. He ended on an upbeat note: "Everyone loves a comeback story. Let's work together to write the best one ever."[8]

Two more key constituencies were the board of directors and the Ford family. Mulally tested the same message with both groups: Ford needed to simplify its product line, produce cars that customers wanted, and develop a clear view of the future. Both groups responded enthusiastically, and many of Henry Ford's descendants happily signed their names on a diagram of the family tree that Mulally had brought with him to their first meeting.

Mulally also understood that Ford needed help from the United Automobile Workers (UAW). Both company and union were in a tough spot. Ford's survival depended on negotiating a lower cost structure in its UAW contracts. The autoworkers' leadership knew that Ford was in deep trouble and feared a disaster for its members if the company failed. Top leadership from both company and union held many meetings, at which Mulally promoted his mantra of "profitable growth for all." His case centered around the fact that Ford was losing money on every car it made in North America. He argued that Ford had only three options: keep losing money and go out of business, move production offshore, or get a union contract that would let them build cars in the United States. The union reluctantly bought the argument, and after many rounds of bargaining and some last-minute high drama, company and union agreed on a deal that enabled Ford to build more cars in America.

Still another critical challenge was getting the support of Ford's senior executives, including some who had hoped to become CEO. The proud, intensely competitive group of longtime Ford veterans was initially unimpressed with the new chief. To some, Mulally seemed like a smiling, overgrown Boy Scout who lacked the smarts, toughness, and gravitas to run Ford. He apparently didn't even know how to dress, showing up in a dark-suit culture wearing a sport coat and olive pants. Many in the room felt that the auto industry was too tough for Mulally to understand, and Ford's chief technical officer put it to him directly: "We appreciate you coming here from a company like Boeing, but you've got to realize that this is a very, very capital-intensive business with long product development lead times. The average car is made up of thousands of different parts, and they all have to work together flawlessly."

"That's really interesting," Mulally replied, with his usual genial smile and unflappable aura. "The typical passenger jet has four million parts, and if just one of them fails, the whole thing can fall out of the sky. So I feel pretty comfortable with this."[9] That quieted the naysayers for the moment, but Mulally knew that much of his team still wondered if he could do the job. Instead of trying to convince them directly, he turned to structural changes to bring clarity and focus to the top team as well as Ford's global operations.

Mulally quickly concluded that Ford needed a major overhaul of a "convoluted management structure riddled with overlapping responsibilities and tangled chains of command."[10] He implemented what had worked for him at Boeing, a matrix structure that crisscrossed the strong regional organizations with upgraded global functional units. So, for example, the head of engineering or quality in Ford Europe would report to both the regional president in Europe and to a global vice president back at headquarters. Mulally wanted strong executives at the head of these global functions, and he wanted them on the top team reporting directly to him. In his view, this was critical because fractionation across units was preventing Ford from leveraging the advantages of its global scale.

Mulally knew that the structure would work only if the top executives came together as a team. He pulled out another structural device he had developed at Boeing: the Business Plan Review (BPR). He replaced dozens of high-level gatherings with one key meeting—same time, same place, every week. Attendance was required, in person or via video hookup, for everyone who reported to him. In the old days, no one wanted to admit that anything was going wrong, so executives ritualistically came to meetings with thick binders and a bevy of assistants to help them hide problems under a blizzard of details.

Mulally changed the rules. Executives now had to make their own five-minute reports, using a standard format, on progress against plan. Mulally asked lots of questions, but told them it was OK if someone didn't know an answer, "Because we'll all be here again next week, and I *know* you'll know it then."[11] Every item in each report had to be color-coded: green for on track, yellow for needs attention, and red for anything that was off plan or behind schedule. "This is the only way I know to operate," he told them. "We need to have everybody involved. We need to have a plan. And we need to know where we are on the plan."[12]

The head of Ford's international operations, Mark Schultz, had hoped to be CEO himself and didn't like the new guy's rules. He dug in his heels. At the first BPR meeting, he said he wanted his chief financial officer to report for him. When Mulally told him he had to do it himself, he did his best, but was obviously unprepared. After a few minutes, Mulally had heard enough and tried to cut him off, but it took four tries before Schultz got the hint. After the meeting, an angry Schultz told Mulally that he would not be able to attend all the BPR meetings because he had important work to do in Asia. With his usual smile, Mulally told him he didn't have to come to the meetings—but couldn't stay on the team if he didn't. Schultz figured he could play by his own rules because his longtime fishing buddy, Bill Ford, would protect him. That was a misjudgment. When Mulally eliminated his job and offered him a smaller one, Schultz decided to retire rather than accept a demotion.

Other executives got the message: Mulally was in charge, and Bill Ford was solidly behind him. As executives began to fall into line, Mulally was able to turn his attention to two pressing human resource issues: talent at the top and morale throughout the company. He respected the overall capabilities of Ford's executives and felt that the company needed continuity rather than massive turnover in the senior leadership. He asked his HR chief to develop retention plans for all the key executives. If he heard that one of them was thinking about leaving, he would drop by his or her office to ask directly, "Are you going to stay?" Usually the executive did. Mulally also needed strong players to lead the newly upgraded global functional units, and he scoured the company to find them.

Mulally's second major HR challenge was rebuilding the commitment and morale of Ford's workforce in a time of downsizing and dismal business results. At headquarters, he was a master of leading by wandering around. He often skipped the executive dining room to eat in the company cafeteria, standing in line with his tray and chatting up accountants or sales analysts. He popped into meetings where he wasn't expected and asked, "What are you guys talking about?" Ford lifers who had waited forever for a CEO who would listen to them started sending emails to Mulally; he answered them all and sometimes followed up with a telephone call.[13] One engineer showed up at Mulally's office with a pile of schematics, including drawings for more than a dozen different hood structures. He wanted to show the new chief just how muddled Ford's design and engineering were. The drawings confirmed what Mulally already suspected. He asked if there was a way to reduce the complexity. When the engineer said yes, Mulally put him in charge of the effort.[14]

To reach the thousands of employees beyond Detroit, Mulally traveled to locations around the world, asking questions and reinforcing the message that Ford was coming back. He issued every employee a wallet card that carried the essence of the plan going forward: "One Ford. One Team. One Plan. One Goal." He loved to pass out the cards every chance he got.[15]

Symbolically, Mulally's biggest challenge was to change the perception that Ford was on a path to oblivion because it had become too bloated, bureaucratic, and self-absorbed to understand or adapt to the realities of the twenty-first century. As he sought a more hopeful story about the future, he followed the lead of wise symbolic leaders such as Lou Gerstner at IBM (whose story we told in Chapter One). He looked back to the past. Mulally combed Ford's corporate archives, believing that a key to Ford's future was a return to the principles that had made it great in the first place. He hit pay dirt with an ad that Henry Ford had run in 1925 in the *Saturday Evening Post* (the most widely read publication in America at the time). Under a picture of an American family standing atop a grassy knoll next to their Model T, the caption read, "Opening the highways to all mankind." In the text, Henry Ford outlined his vision: "A whole-hearted belief that riding on the people's highways should be within easy reach of all the people."[16] That ad gave Mulally the touchstone he was looking for. He wrote stream-of-consciousness notes about what needed to happen: pull stakeholders together, form tight relationships with the board and the Ford family, respect the heritage, implement reliable discipline and a business plan, and include everyone. Then he took another sheet of paper and sketched his "Alan Legacy":[17]

- Clear, compelling vision going forward
- Survive the perfect storm
- Develop a profitable growth plan, global products, and product strategy
- A skilled and motivated team
- Reliable, ongoing Business Plan Review process
- A leader and leadership team with "One Ford" vision and implementation tenacity

"One Ford" may sound simple, even simplistic, but for Mulally it was a powerful mantra and polestar. He never tired of repeating and reinforcing the message. It meant replacing chaos, parochialism, and political infighting with simplicity, teamwork, and unity—worldwide.

Mulally's efforts worked, though more slowly than he had initially hoped. Just as Ford began to turn the corner, the recession of 2008 devastated the auto industry worldwide. But Ford was better prepared than its crosstown rivals. Mulally, Bill Ford, and Ford's chief financial officer had made a prescient decision in 2006 to bet the company by borrowing all the money they could—some $24 billion. They foresaw that Ford's credit rating would get weaker and the borrowing window might close if the economy tanked. General Motors CEO Rick Wagoner told them they were crazy and would regret the decision.

But two years later, the economic crisis forced both General Motors and Chrysler to beg for U.S. government bailouts to stay in business. Ford had the cushion it needed to avoid taking taxpayers' money. That became a huge marketing edge. After losing market share for thirteen straight years, Ford gained share in 2009, turned a profit in 2010, and achieved its highest profits in more than a decade in 2011. Mulally turned sixty-five in 2011 amid speculation about when he would retire. Board chair Bill Ford expressed the hope that he would stay forever, and Ford announced late in 2012 that Mulally would stay in his job at least until 2014.

Mulally's achievements at both Boeing and Ford have earned him a reputation as one of the great turnaround leaders in business history. He did it by seeing and responding to key issues in every frame. Politically, he recognized the need to negotiate workable agreements with all the many stakeholders whose support was vital and whose opposition could have been fatal. He created many venues for airing differences, building relationships, and crafting agreements that gave him the support and resources he needed to move forward.

In terms of structure, he recognized that Ford's existing architecture was preventing it from taking full advantage of the talent of its people and the strength of its brand. He developed a simpler, tighter global structure and implemented new processes for the top team that clarified where Ford was going and how it would get there.

On the human resource front, Mulally became a coach who recognized the importance of talent in key positions and of morale throughout the ranks. He asked questions, listened, made communications more transparent, and helped restore employees' pride in their company.

Symbolically, Mulally recognized that constituents both inside and outside the company needed something to hang on to while sailing through the turbulence. He went back in time to legendary founder Henry Ford to identify and resurrect beliefs and principles that had once made Ford great. Like other great symbolic leaders, he updated a historic legacy, creating the mantra of "One Ford." He became the storyteller and healer providing historical roots, direction, and inspiration going forward.

CONCLUSION

Innovation inevitably generates issues that reveal the limits of a leader's control. In implementing necessary changes, leaders can make a difference, but they need to attune their strategy to a comprehensive understanding of their organization's circumstances. Sometimes, an organization needs fresh ideas and strategies from outside, but leaders often have a better chance if they look within an organization for ideas and energy. The frames can help leaders think ahead, anticipating obstacles to change: incompetence, confusion, conflict, and loss. Each lens also provides support by guiding leaders in responding to those challenges. Leaders who can move fluidly across the roles of coach, architect, politician, and healer can address the full range of challenges that any change effort will encounter. They are the leaders who, like Alan Mulally, can see what needs to happen and orchestrate a change process that gets it done.

Searching for Soul
Leadership Ethics

The frames or leadership lenses help leaders think better and make better decisions. But many of the decisions they face require choosing among imperfect options. This is the kind of situation that James E. Burke, CEO of Johnson & Johnson (J&J), faced in 1982 when news arrived that bottles of Tylenol, one of the company's most profitable products, had been poisoned. On the one hand, he could pull the product from store shelves at a huge cost; on the other, he could take the chance that the tampering incident had been limited to the few bottles that were discovered. But then more people could die. Burke decided to pull the product, because a value in the J&J Credo calls for putting people—"doctors, nurses, hospitals, mothers, and all others we serve"—ahead of corporate profits.

Burke's dilemma is an example of deeper existential questions that lie beyond the important leadership tasks of thinking and doing. What ethical ideals will inform your leadership? What faith will sustain you through the inevitable dilemmas, frustrations, and vicissitudes you will face? Each of the frames can help you understand how organizations work, but each also embodies a philosophy about what's significant—about values and soul as well as effectiveness.

Companies swept up in ethics scandals year after year often seem to have lost touch with any values beyond the "morals of the marketplace," which often translate to no morals at all. Recent examples of companies that have apparently gone adrift of their ethical moorings include Rupert Murdoch's media empire (phone hacking); Wal-Mart (bribing officials in Mexico); an investment company in Japan ($2 billion fraud); many of the world's big, brand-name banks (manipulating interest rates, deceiving customers, stone-walling investigators, and so on); and J&J (putting profits ahead of patients).

Thirty years after the Tylenol crisis, J&J continued to display the Credo on its website, proclaiming proudly, "Our Credo is more than just a moral compass. We believe it's a recipe for business success." But by 2012, a series of lawsuits, product recalls, and customer complaints suggested that the Credo was at risk of becoming more lip service than serious commitment. In 2010 and again in 2012, the company had to recall children's Tylenol. In 2011, J&J pleaded guilty to bribing European doctors. In 2012, judges in multiple states ordered J&J and a subsidiary to pay fines totaling some $2 billion for minimizing or hiding the dangers associated with an antipsychotic drug. The *New York Times* reported that "consumer confidence in Johnson & Johnson, once one of the most trusted brands, has dipped in recent years as the company recalled dozens of products, including millions of bottles of children's Tylenol and other medications, as well as artificial hips and other products."[1]

Where did J&J go astray? When a business has similar problems across different units and even different continents, the signs point to the leadership—in this case to CEO William Weldon, who earned a spot on multiple lists of the worst CEOs of the year in 2010 and 2011. Inside the company, Weldon was viewed as "a tough competitor who hates to lose," but he did not engender the kind of veneration that J&J employees had for his predecessors, James E. Burke and Ralph Larsen.[2] Management professor Eric Gordon observed, "There was a time when people really believed in [the Credo] and took great pride in it. But those days are long gone."[3] Gordon saw Weldon's relentless focus on the bottom line as the source of the company's many woes. "Bill Weldon sets the priorities and the culture for the company," he said, and the problems reflect "people trying to get their bonuses, hit their numbers and keep their job."

Contemporary business leaders often experience brutal pressures for short-term results and shareholder value, which too often lead them to lose sight of a simple truth: drifting away from your ethical core carries many costs, financial as well as personal and spiritual.

SOUL AND SPIRIT IN ORGANIZATIONS

What J&J lost becomes clear if we compare it to the medical devices giant Medtronic. Like J&J, Medtronic states its core purpose as serving patients rather than shareholders. Its CEO from 1989 to 2001, Bill George, is an advocate of authentic leadership and critic of short-term thinking. His position on Medtronic's mission was clear: "Medtronic is *not* in the business to maximize shareholder value. We *are* in business to maximize value to the patients we serve."[4] This principle was rooted in Medtronic's original mission statement, developed by founder Earl Bakken in the 1960s. To reinforce the message, Bakken created the "Mission and Medallion Ceremony." He met personally with every new employee, reviewed the mission, shared stories of how it played out in practice, and gave the employee a bronze medallion that carried an image of a patient rising from the operating table and walking into a full life. That tradition continued even as Medtronic grew much larger. During his term as CEO, Bill George conducted medallion ceremonies for thousands of employees around the world—sometimes at 2 A.M. for night-shift workers.

Do such noble sentiments make a difference in practice? Bill George thought so. In one case, shortly after he promoted a very talented executive to head Medtronic's European operations, George learned that the individual was maintaining a secret account in a Swiss bank, presumably for making payments to doctors. When George asked him about it, the executive argued that American values shouldn't be imposed in Europe. Not American values, George responded, but Medtronic values, and they were the same everywhere. Although it was painful, he asked the executive to resign, released details to regulators in both the United States and Europe, and publicized the incident so that people inside and outside the company understood Medtronic's unyielding ethical position.

How did Medtronic's squeaky clean approach work out for shareholders? During George's tenure, Medtronic's share price increased at a rate of 36 percent per year, and its market capitalization rose from $1 billion to $60 billion. Of course, there were other fast-growth companies operating in the same period. Enron and WorldCom, for example, also shot up very fast—only to crash into bankruptcy in 2001, the same year Bill George retired from Medtronic, which kept right on growing.

Some people have such strong ethical convictions that it matters little where they work, but most of us are at greater risk of losing our way. We are social beings, attuned to cues and expectations from our workplace and our colleagues about what to do in the face of moral dilemmas. In recent years, one organization after another has lost its soul in the race for innovation, growth, a rising share price, and big paychecks. An organization that loses track of any redeeming moral purpose cannot provide credible ethical guardrails for its employees. The results are often painful.

Can an organization have soul? Many doubt it, but there is growing evidence that it is a critical element in long-run success. A dictionary definition of *soul* uses terms such as "animating force," "immaterial essence," and "spiritual nature." For an organization, group, or family, soul can also be viewed as a resolute sense of character, a deep confidence about who we are, what we care about, and what we deeply believe in. J&J had it, but lost it. Medtronic kept it and prospered. Leadership makes the difference.

In forcing out the European executive with the Swiss bank account, Bill George demonstrated two key characteristics of leaders with soul: clarity about values, and willingness to act on them even when faced with a painful moral quandary. Ask yourself how clear you are about your own values as a leader. What values do you hold dear? Could you summarize them in a brief, personal credo? Every leader and organization needs to choose and commit to personal and collective ethical principles. We believe that the frames can offer guidance and stimulate reflection for leaders who aspire to create spiritually anchored communities. Each frame implies both a central value and a leadership "gift" that can help breathe soul into an organization's daily life. Exhibit 13.1 summarizes our view.

Exhibit 13.1.
Reframing Ethics

Frame	Leadership Ethic	Leader's Contribution
Structural	Excellence	Authorship
Human resource	Caring	Love
Political	Justice	Power
Symbolic	Faith	Significance

THE FACTORY: EXCELLENCE AND AUTHORSHIP

The structural frame, with its emphasis on finding the right design for the task at hand, implies a value of excellence. Almost every leader and organization strives for excellence, but flawed products and mediocre services keep reminding us that the hunt does not always bag the quarry. One reason is that excellence requires more than pious sermons from top management. It demands commitment at all levels of an enterprise. How do leaders foster such dedication? As we have put it elsewhere, "Leading is giving. Leadership is an ethic, a gift of oneself."[5] Critical for creating and maintaining excellence is the gift of what we refer to as authorship:

> Authorship turns the classic organizational pyramid on its side and provides space within boundaries. Leaders increase their influence and build more productive organizations. Workers experience the satisfactions of creativity, craftsmanship, and a job well done. Authorship transcends the traditional adversarial relationship in which superiors try to increase control while subordinates resist them at every turn. Trusting people to solve problems generates higher levels of motivation and better solutions. The leader's responsibility is to create conditions that promote authorship. Individuals need to see their work as meaningful and worthwhile, to feel personally accountable for the consequences of their efforts, and to get feedback that lets them know the results.[6]

Southwest Airlines and Zappos offer two compelling examples of authorship. In both, associates are encouraged to be themselves, have fun, and use their sense of humor. On Southwest you might hear required FAA safety briefings sung to the music of a popular song or delivered as a stand-up comedy routine. ("Those of you who wish to smoke will please file out to our lounge on the wing, where you can enjoy our feature film, *Gone with the Wind*.") Too frivolous for something as serious as a safety announcement? Just the opposite: it's a way to get passengers to pay attention to a message they usually ignore. It's also a very good way for flight attendants to have fun and feel creative rather than being mechanically scripted by mandated routine.

THE FAMILY: CARING AND LOVE

A central theme of the human resource frame—improving the fit between the individual and the organization—is possible only when leaders care about the people they lead. Caring—one person's compassion and concern for another—is the primary purpose and the ethical glue that holds a family together. A compassionate family or community requires servant-leaders concerned with the needs and wishes of members and stakeholders. This commitment to caring creates a challenging obligation for leaders to understand and to safeguard the collective well-being. The gift of the servant-leader is love.

Love is largely absent from most modern corporations. Few managers would use the word in any context more profound than their feelings about food, family, films, or games. They shy away from love's deeper meanings, fearing both its power and its risks. Caring begins with knowing; it requires listening, understanding, and accepting. It progresses through a deepening sense of appreciation, respect, and ultimately love.

People talk openly about love at Southwest Airlines. As former president Colleen Barrett reminisced, "Love is a word that isn't used often in Corporate America, but we used it at Southwest from the beginning." The word *love* is woven into the culture. They fly out of Love Field in Dallas; their symbol on the New York Stock Exchange is LUV; the employee newsletter is called *Luv Lines*; and their twentieth anniversary slogan was "Twenty Years of Loving You."[7] They hold an annual "Heroes of the Heart" ceremony to honor members of the Southwest family who have gone above and beyond even Southwest's high call of duty. There are, of course, ups and downs in any family, and the airline industry certainly experiences both. Through life's peaks and valleys, love holds people—both employees and passengers—together in a caring community.

In the first month after Marilyn Carlson Nelson joined the Carlson Companies, the travel and entertainment conglomerate (including, for example, Radisson and TGI Friday's) her father had founded, she went with him to hear MBA students from the University of Minnesota talk about the Carlson business. She asked them how they saw the company. At first, no one wanted to answer. Finally, one student said it was perceived as a sweatshop that didn't care about people. She decided at that moment that the company's culture had to change. When she became CEO, she set out to create a company that "cared for customers by creating the most caring environment for its employees."[8]

A key test of that commitment came on 9/11, three years after she became CEO. Aviation was grounded, and the travel industry was in a state of chaos. Carlson got on the phone with the company's leadership from around the world and told them just to make decisions based on the credo: take care of your employees first, your customers second, your competitors' customers next, and, finally, anything you can do for the community. She was amazed at the outpouring of energy and creativity. A hotel near the Twin Towers turned its ballroom into a relief station that provided food and shelter for first responders.[9] Amid the trauma of 9/11, "Carlsonians" felt a sense of empowerment and pride that they were able to do something positive.

For those who see caring as a distraction or a dubious investment, organizations such as Southwest Airlines and the Carlson Companies demonstrate a simple truth: if you care about your people, they are much more likely to care about you—and their work.

THE JUNGLE: JUSTICE AND POWER

Politics and politicians are routinely viewed as objects of scorn—often for good reason. Is there any ethical consideration associated with the political frame? We believe there is: a commitment to justice. In a world of competing interests and scarce resources, leaders are continually compelled to make trade-offs. They cannot give everyone everything they want, but they can honor a value of fairness in making decisions about who gets what. Robert C. Solomon sees justice as the ultimate virtue in corporations, because fairness—the perception that employees, customers, and investors are all getting their due—is the glue that holds things together.[10] Nothing is more corrosive in a family, an organization, or a society than a widespread perception that corruption is undermining fairness.

Justice is often hard to define, and disagreement about its application is inevitable. The key gift that leaders can offer in pursuit of justice is power—the capacity for constituents to make a difference in things they care about. People with a voice in key decisions are far more likely to feel a sense of fairness because they had a say and they better understand how the decision was made. Leaders who hoard power produce powerless organizations. People stripped of power look for ways to fight back: passive resistance, withdrawal, sabotage, or angry militancy. Giving power liberates energy for more productive use. If people have a sense of efficacy and an ability to influence their surroundings, they are more likely to direct their energy and intelligence toward making a contribution instead of making trouble. In their excellent book *The Idea-Driven Organization*, Alan Robinson and Dean Schroeder mount a compelling case for the contributions frontline workers can make when management listens to their ideas, instead of issuing top-down instructions to do things the workers know are wrong.[11]

During the Reagan administration, House Speaker "Tip" O'Neill was a constant thorn in the side of the president. O'Neill called Reagan "a cheerleader for selfishness." Reagan returned the shot by comparing O'Neill to Pac-Man: "a round thing that consumes money." But Reagan also spoke at a fundraiser to support the O'Neill Library at Boston College,[12] and they carved out a mutually just agreement: they would fight ferociously for their independent interests, but stay civil and find fairness wherever possible. They had a rule: "After six o'clock, we're friends, whatever divisiveness the political battle has produced during working hours." Both men gave each other the gift of power. During one acrimonious public debate between the two, Regan reportedly whispered, "Tip, can we pretend it's six o'clock?"[13]

Power and authorship are related; autonomy, space, and freedom are important in both. Still, there is an important distinction between the two. Artists, authors, and craftspeople can experience authorship while working alone. Power, in contrast, is meaningful only in relation to others. It is the capacity to wield influence and get things to happen on a broader scale.

The gift of power is important at multiple levels. As individuals, people want the power to control their immediate environment and the factors that impinge directly on them. Many traditional workplaces still suffocate their employees with time clocks, rigid rules, and authoritarian bosses. A global challenge at the group level is responding to ethnic, racial, cultural, and gender diversity. Gallos, Ramsey, and colleagues get to the heart of this issue: "Systems are most often designed by dominant group members to meet their own needs,"[14] which often means they systematically exclude others who are not "like us."

Justice requires that leaders seek to empower the powerless—ensuring access to decision making, creating internal advocacy groups, building diversity into information and incentive systems, and strengthening career opportunities.[15] All this happens only with a rock-solid commitment from top management.

Justice also has important implications for the increasingly urgent question of sustainability: How long can a production or business process last before it collapses as a result of the resource depletion or environmental damage it produces? Decisions about sustainability inevitably involve trade-offs among the interests of constituencies that differ in role, place, and time. How do we balance our company's profitability against damage to the environment, or current concerns against those of future generations? Organizations with a commitment to justice will take these dilemmas seriously and look for ways to engage and empower diverse stakeholders in making choices.

THE TEMPLE: FAITH AND SIGNIFICANCE

The central theme of the symbolic frame is the way humans discover and create meaning in an ambiguous and chaotic world. Leaders can build and sustain meaning by fostering faith in an organization and its work. Like a temple, an organization can be seen as a sacred place, an expression of human aspirations and hope, a monument to faith in human possibility. A temple is a gathering place for a community of people with shared traditions, values, and beliefs. Members of a community may be diverse in many ways (age, background, economic status, personal interests), but they are tied together by shared faith and bonded by a sanctified spiritual covenant. In work organizations, faith is strengthened if individuals feel that the organization is characterized by such durable values as excellence, caring, and justice. Above all, people must believe that the organization is doing something worth doing—fulfilling a calling that adds value to the world.

Significance is partly about the work itself, but even more about how the work is embraced. This point is made by an old story about three stonemasons giving an account of their work. The first said that he was cutting stone. The second said that he was building a cathedral. The third said simply that he was "serving God."

Temples need spiritual leaders. This does not mean leaders who promote religion or a particular theology, but leaders who bring a genuine concern for the human spirit. The dictionary defines spirit as "the intelligent or immaterial part of man," "the animating or vital principal in living things," and "the moral nature of humanity." Spiritual leaders help people find meaning, hope, and faith in work and help them answer fundamental questions that have confronted humans of every time and place: Who am I as an individual? Who are we as a people? What is the purpose of my life, of our collective existence? What ethical principles should we follow? What legacy will we leave?

Spiritual leaders offer the gift of significance, rooted in confidence that the work is precious, that devotion and loyalty to a beloved institution can offer hard-to-emulate intangible rewards. Work is exhilarating and joyful at its best, and arduous, frustrating, and exhausting in less happy moments. Many adults embark on their careers with enthusiasm, confidence, and a desire to make a contribution. Some never lose that spark, but too many do. They become frustrated with sterile or toxic working conditions and discouraged by how hard it is to make a difference or even to know if they have made one. Tracy Kidder puts it well in writing about teachers: "Good teachers put snags in the river of children passing by, and over time, they redirect hundreds of lives. There is an innocence that conspires to hold humanity together, and it is made up of people who can never fully know the good they have done."[16] The gift of significance helps people sustain their faith rather than burn out and abandon work that has lost its meaning.

Significance is built through the use of many expressive and symbolic forms: rituals, ceremonies, stories, and music. An organization without a rich symbolic life grows empty and barren. The magic of special occasions is vital in building significance into collective life. Medtronic's Mission and Medallion ceremony for new employees offers a simple but powerful example. The presence of the CEO, the sharing of stories, and the gift of the bronze medallion all speak to the significance of the work and the faith that sustains it, while adding symbolic depth and magic to a new employee's induction process.

During Burke's reign as CEO of Johnson & Johnson, his concern that the Credo might become mere window dressing prompted him to initiate a series of meetings he called the Credo Challenge. He brought in managers and told them, "If you do not believe in the Credo, and you aren't urging your employees to abide by it, then it is an act of pretension. In that case, you should take it off the wall of your office and throw it away."[17] The process stimulated thought and debate that ultimately revitalized the company's commitment to its time-honored values. Burke's concern that the credo would decay into window dressing seemed justified more recently during Bill Weldon's tenure as CEO. Even though Weldon insisted that Johnson & Johnson was still committed to its Credo, a series of scandals made it clear that something had been lost along the way.

When ceremony and ritual are authentic and attuned, they fire the imagination, evoke insight, and touch the heart. Ceremony weaves past, present, and future into life's tapestry. Ritual helps us face and comprehend life's everyday shocks, triumphs, and mysteries. Both help us experience the unseen web of significance that ties a community together. When inauthentic, such occasions become meaningless, repetitious, and alienating— wasting our time, disconnecting us from work, and splintering us from one another. "Community must become more than just gathering the troops, telling the stories, and remembering things past. Community must also be rooted in values that do not fail, values that go beyond the self-aggrandizement of human leaders."[18]

Stories give flesh to shared values and sacred beliefs. Everyday life in organizations brings many heartwarming moments and dramatic encounters. Transformed into stories, these events fill an organization's treasure chest with lore and legend. Told and retold, they draw people together and connect them with the significance of their work. Lou Gerstner at IBM and Alan Mulally at Ford both found inspiration in the stories of legendary founders—Thomas J. Watson Sr. and Henry Ford—who had built great businesses decades earlier.

Max De Pree, famed both as both a business leader and an author of elegant books on leadership, underscored the role of faith in business: "Being faithful is more important than being successful. Corporations can and should have a redemptive purpose. We need to weigh the pragmatic in the clarifying light of the moral. We must understand that reaching our potential is more important than reaching our goals."[19] Spiritual leaders have the responsibility of sustaining and encouraging faith in themselves and in recalling others to the faith when they have wandered from it or lost it.

CONCLUSION

Ethics ultimately must be rooted in soul: an organization's commitment to its deeply rooted identity, beliefs, and values. Each leadership lens offers a perspective on the ethical responsibilities of organizations and the moral authority of leaders. Every organization needs to evolve a profound sense of its own ethical and spiritual core. The frames offer spiritual guidelines for the quest.

Signs are everywhere that institutions around the world suffer from a crisis of meaning and moral authority. Rapid change, high mobility, globalization, and racial, cultural, and ethnic conflict tear at the fabric of community. Leaders cannot escape the responsibility to track budgets, motivate people, respond to political pressures, and attend to culture, but they serve a deeper, more powerful, and more enduring role if they are models and catalysts for such values as excellence, caring, justice, and faith.

Great Leaders, Great Stories

A s you think so shall you lead. Much of the literature on leadership, as well as courses and programs to develop leaders, focuses on the style, attributes, or actions of leaders. That makes sense, because we expect leaders to get things done. But thinking needs to precede action. Otherwise, action is a shot in the dark by mindless leaders who haven't thought enough about why they are choosing one path or another. The quality of leaders' thinking depends ultimately on the stories they tell. Drawing lessons from life experiences, all leaders weave stories over time that they carry with them wherever they go. Even though sometimes demeaned, "war stories" are the living literature, the lore of leadership. Leaders live within the stories they have created, and invite others to join them on the adventure.

Human lives are packed with stories. We get them from books, newspapers, movies, and TV shows and from swapping tales with friends in person or online. When we're not taking in the stories of others, we're spinning our own. We daydream while awake, and at night our dreams are filled with strange, wondrous, or terrifying tales.[1]

Storytelling is our most basic and powerful form of communication. It transmits emotionally charged information in a form that is accessible, attractive, and memorable to others. Stories are also a basic form of social glue, bonding groups and organizations together through historical legends and memorable tales.

WORLDVIEWS, FRAMES, AND STORIES

Figure 14.1 presents a model of how leaders interact with the world around them. A leader appears, bringing a worldview and a personal story to a particular time and place. The setting provides a context with its own organizational story. The leader's worldview and personal story influence how she responds to the organization's story. She may hear and appreciate or ignore or discount or misread the narrative of her new locale. However she makes sense of the organization's story and circumstances, she constructs a narrative to guide her and the organization going forward. Then she asks constituents to become participants in a shared story. When Alan Mulally, for example (Chapter Twelve), arrived at Ford as the new CEO in 2006, he brought with him a worldview and a personal story acquired over his lifetime, including his many years in leadership roles at Boeing. He quickly concluded that Ford had lost touch with its own story and identity, and set

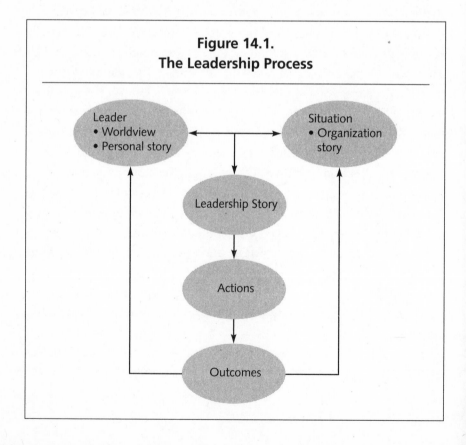

**Figure 14.1.
The Leadership Process**

Leader
• Worldview
• Personal story

Situation
• Organization story

Leadership Story

Actions

Outcomes

to work to engage constituents in a revival of a great drama that went back to the legend of Henry Ford.

The Leader's Worldview

We can think of a leader's worldview as containing four key elements that influence how he or she makes sense of the world:

1. **Concepts and categories: What's out there? What are the ideas and things I might notice and pay attention to?**

Leaders need mental models with enough breadth and depth to help them see and make sense out of the most important elements of their situation. We saw in Chapter Eleven, for example, that Amazon founder Jeff Bezos has a rich and deep palette of concepts in the areas of structure, process, and metrics, but a much sparser set of human resource concepts. It is not surprising that Amazon is at the frontier in areas where Bezos is strong and struggles in the areas that he is weak. Bezos is one of the world's most admired business leaders, but his company is not likely to appear on lists of best places to work. Media accounts of Amazon's human resource practices are usually highly critical. A basic point of this book is that the four frames or leadership lenses can guide leaders in recognizing where their own mental models are rich or impoverished.

2. **Beliefs: How do things work? What actions lead to what outcomes?**

Even if leaders see what they need to see, they act on the basis of their beliefs about causality: What will happen if I do one thing or another? We saw an example of this in Chapter Four with Ricardo Semler. After he took over his father's company, his initial effort to fix things relied on a belief that tighter structure and more elaborate controls would produce better results. This approach worked at first, but ultimately became self-defeating. Semler then went in search of something different, and gradually developed a philosophy that achieved extraordinary results for him, built around the premise that if you empower workers and tap their wisdom, they will accomplish things you never thought possible. Jeff Bezos believes that success comes from ignoring Wall Street's advice and investing in anything that will improve the customer experience. Howard Schultz sees passion for coffee and community as the bedrock of his company's remarkable growth. In contrast, Ron Johnson's beliefs led him astray—the new, hipper JCPenney's stores he created alienated old customers without attracting new ones.

3. Values: What's good or bad? What's important or not?

One of Ricardo Semler's first experiments was to eliminate the practice of searching employees on their way out the door to make sure they weren't stealing anything from the plant. He had decided that trust was vital and that it didn't matter much if theft went up or down. Conversely, Jeff Bezos coddles his customers but not his employees because the customer experience tops his priority list, while employee satisfaction lags far behind.

4. Self-image: Who am I? What do I care about? What are my leadership strengths and weaknesses?

Self-awareness is a vital skill for leaders; without it they will have difficulty understanding or anticipating how their constituents see and respond to them. Ron Johnson's habit of using one-way video links as a preferred medium for communicating with JCPenney employees distanced him and made it hard for him to get feedback that he was losing credibility with the troops. A year later, it's hard to know what he learned from the experience, but he told one journalist that the accounts of his tenure there were "lacking in depth, largely inaccurate, and surprisingly uninformed."[2]

The Leader's Story

Consciously or not, leaders create a personal leadership story to guide their work, a story built over the course of a lifetime's experience. Organizations also fabricate a story, gleaned from their past and adapted to present circumstances. A manager of a Ritz-Carlton Hotel remarked, "It's hard to be a legend without a great story." Some organizations maintain connections to their roots; others lose contact and become rootless.

As new leaders assume their roles, a dialogue opens, an interplay between the leader's story and that of the organization. New questions come to the surface:

1. Where have we been?

2. Where are we now?

3. Where should we go from here?

4. How will we get there?

Alan Mulally's remarkable turnaround at Ford provides a particularly clear and instructive example. Mulally arrived at Ford with a story shaped on his way up the ranks to the number-two position at Boeing. His worldview was rich in concepts from all four frames, with a particularly strong respect for history and culture. His self-image combined low-key Midwestern humility with quiet confidence, strong intellect, and the courage to take on impossible missions. He held a set of beliefs about what worked that he had honed over his years at Boeing, in an industry that presented challenges much like those at Ford.

Mulally was clear-eyed about the problems at Ford, including a weak product line, excessive bureaucracy, political infighting, lack of direction, a cash crunch, and a skid toward bankruptcy. As soon as he took the job, Mulally began the task of blending his own story with the current narrative at Ford. Like other great leaders, Mulally worked quickly but systematically, building a new, historically anchored storyline and testing it as he went along. He knew that Ford people had a pressing need for a narrative that provided guidance and reassurance, but he also knew that the tale had to make sense and point in the right direction.

He studied Ford's history and used it to construct a core message: Ford would once again become the company that Henry Ford would want it to be. He distilled that into the mantra of "One Ford," which implied a leaner, simpler, more focused, and unified company that would leverage its global assets to build cars people wanted at prices they were willing to pay. His story of "how we'll get there" included significant initiatives on multiple fronts. He invested substantial personal capital in building relationships with the many constituents whose support was vital. He worked with the United Automobile Workers union to agree on a new contract that let Ford sell cars made in the United States at a profit. He made a risky decision to max out Ford's credit card, accumulating cash that enabled Ford to avoid a government bailout when GM and Chrysler both had to take their begging bowls to Washington. He sold off storied European car lines such as Jaguar in order to focus on the Ford brand. He put in new structures and processes designed to reduce bureaucracy while producing more transparency and unity. When fearful employees asked if Ford was going to make it, he told them, "We have a plan, and the plan says we are going to make it."[3]

Contrast Mulally's success at Ford with Ron Johnson's short and tragic era at JCPenney (see Chapter One). Johnson arrived at JCPenney with a story he had evolved during successful leadership stints at Target and the Apple Stores. He seemed like an ideal candidate to shed JCPenney's image as a tired brand with aging customers. His story sounded plausible and exciting: JCPenney would eliminate the confusing flood of phony sales and coupons and become an exciting destination retailer where hip consumers could sip a latte and have their kids entertained.

Why did he fail? Johnson skipped the key step of testing his story against JCPenney's circumstances. His narrative was conjured up in the hip environs of California's Silicon Valley, and seemed ill-suited for a mid-market retailer based in Texas. Johnson spent little time in the stores or at the Dallas headquarters, sometimes communicating to JCPenney staff via videocasts from his home in Palo Alto. Because Apple didn't do market testing, he figured JCPenney didn't need to either. Even as sales fell and customers deserted, Johnson kept insisting that he was on the right track, seemingly oblivious to the disaster that was unfolding in the stores.

The divorce that finally ended the marriage of Ron Johnson and JCPenney could have been avoided. Johnson never seemed to grasp the essence of JCPenney's story. The company had been in decline and needed a creative, successful merchant—someone with Ron Johnson's track record—to make the stores relevant in a fast-moving retail environment. Johnson could have moved to Texas, immersed himself in the JCPenney stores, exchanged ideas with veteran staff, and taken the time to test and evolve his story. But Johnson was so sure of his narrative that he didn't see the need for any of that. As happens for so many leaders, Johnson's attachment to his story and unwillingness to learn from JCPenney's history did him in.

Leaders' stories exchange energy with an organization's story, present and past. Lou Gerstner's story on arrival as IBM's new CEO was that of a hard-nosed strategic thinker. He inherited a company commonly seen as a "bloated whale" whose fortunes were sinking fast. The old IBM, recognized in some leadership circles as a "national treasure," was fading. Gerstner mounted a search for the glories of the past.

He discovered a cultural icon in the person of Thomas J. Watson Sr., whose story cast a long silhouette on the fledgling enterprise: "It was a magical time and Thomas Watson Sr. was the wizard who waved the magic wand, creating the enchantment and excitement."[4] Over subsequent decades, Watson's magic and values dissipated, giving way to a stodgy, inward-looking bureaucracy. Gerstner recognized this and resurrected relevant parts of Watson's story and values to reenergize the company.

By all accounts, Gerstner himself was a gifted storyteller and used stories to illuminate IBM's past, present, and future:

> It was a meeting on Wall Street where Lou Gerstner, the CEO of IBM, met the market analysts . . . So we go into a room and there are people from the various banks and the brokers and the analysts and Gerstner starts telling them stories. Stories about IBM. Stories about the future of IBM. These were stories. He couldn't tell them facts about the future. He was telling them what IBM was going to do. It was all stories. And it worked. It really worked.[5]

CONCLUSION

Great leadership begins when a leader's worldview and personal story, honed over years of experience, meet a situation that presents both challenges and opportunities. Great leaders use multiple frames so as to see what they need to see, and craft a story about what will work. Meanwhile, organizations have evolved their own narratives. The interplay of leaders' and organizations' stories gives rise to an emerging script that, at its best, provides a compelling image of where a group or organization is, where it needs to go, and how it will get there. The story serves as a drama in which both leader and constituents become actors. Great leaders test and evolve their story over time, experimenting, polishing, abandoning plot lines that don't work, and reinforcing those that do. Bad stories often lead to disaster, but good ones conjure magic.

APPENDIX: LEADERSHIP ORIENTATIONS

This questionnaire asks you to describe yourself as a manager and leader. For each item, assign the number 4 to the phrase that best describes you, 3 to the item that is next best, and on down to 1 for the item that is least like you. You can also take the assessment online at http://www.josseybassbusiness.com/2013/07/assessment-leadership-orientations-self-assessment.html.

1. My strongest skills are

    _____ a. Analytical skills

    _____ b. Interpersonal skills

    _____ c. Political skills

    _____ d. Flair for drama

2. The best way to describe me is

    _____ a. Technical expert

    _____ b. Good listener

    _____ c. Skilled negotiator

    _____ d. Inspirational leader

3. What has helped me the most to be successful is my ability to

_____ a. Make good decisions

_____ b. Coach and develop people

_____ c. Build strong alliances and a power base

_____ d. Inspire and excite others

4. What people are most likely to notice about me is my

_____ a. Attention to detail

_____ b. Concern for people

_____ c. Ability to succeed in the face of conflict and opposition

_____ d. Charisma

5. My most important leadership trait is

_____ a. Clear, logical thinking

_____ b. Caring and support for others

_____ c. Toughness and aggressiveness

_____ d. Imagination and creativity

6. I am best described as

_____ a. An analyst

_____ b. A humanist

_____ c. A politician

_____ d. A visionary

SCORING AND INTERPRETATION
Computing Scores

Compute your scores as follows:

ST = 1a + 2a + 3a + 4a + 5a + 6a
HR = 1b + 2b + 3b + 4b + 5b + 6b
PL = 1c + 2c + 3c + 4c + 5c + 6c

$SY = 1d + 2d + 3d + 4d + 5d + 6d$

ST _____   HR _____   PL _____   SY _____   Total _____

The total should be 60; if not, check your work.

Interpreting Scores

The Leadership Orientations instrument is keyed to four different conceptions of organizations and of the task of organizational leadership.

Plot each of your scores on the appropriate axis of the chart in Figure A.1: ST for Structural, HR for Human Resource, PL for Political, and SY for Symbolic. Then read the brief description of each of these orientations toward leadership and organizations.

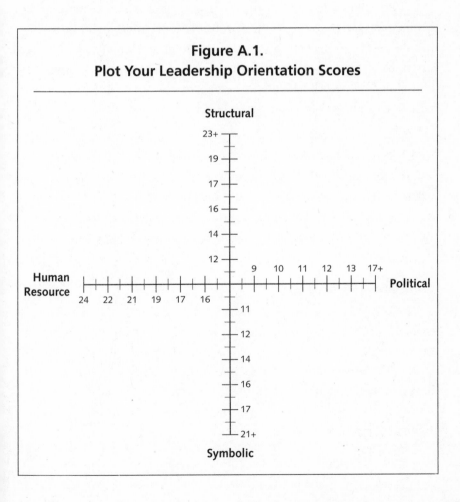

Figure A.1.
Plot Your Leadership Orientation Scores

1. Structural leaders emphasize rationality, analysis, logic, facts, and data. They are likely to believe strongly in the importance of clear structure and well-developed management systems. A good leader is someone who thinks clearly, makes the right decisions, has good analytical skills, and can design structures and systems that get the job done.

2. Human resource leaders emphasize the importance of people. They endorse the view that the central task of management is to develop a good fit between people and organizations. They believe in the importance of coaching, participation, motivation, teamwork, and good interpersonal relations. A good leader is a facilitator and participative manager who supports and empowers others.

3. Political leaders believe that managers and leaders live in a world of conflict and scarce resources. The central task of management is to mobilize the resources needed to advocate and fight for the unit's or the organization's goals and objectives. Political leaders emphasize the importance of building a power base: allies, networks, coalitions. A good leader is an advocate and negotiator who understands politics and is comfortable with conflict.

4. Symbolic leaders believe that the essential task of management is to provide vision and inspiration. They rely on personal charisma and a flair for drama to get people excited and committed to the organizational mission. A good leader is a prophet and visionary, who uses symbols, tells stories, and frames experience in ways that give people hope and meaning.

Comparison Scores

The following table shows percentiles for each frame, based on a sample of more than seven hundred managers from business, education, and government. The scales in Figure A.1 have been adjusted to represent percentile scores. The lowest number for each frame represents the 25th percentile; the highest number represents the 90th percentile. For the structural frame, for example, 25 percent of managers rate themselves 12 or below, and only 10 percent rate themselves 22 or above.

In a sample of more than 700 managers:	Structural	Human Resource	Political	Symbolic
10% rated themselves at or above:	22	24	17	21
25% rated themselves above:	19	22	13	17
50% rated themselves above:	16	19	11	14
75% rated themselves above:	12	16	9	11

NOTES

Part 1

1. Brand, R. "Russell Brand on Revolution: 'We No Longer Have the Luxury of Tradition.'" *New Statesman*, Oct. 24, 2013. http://www.newstatesman.com/politics/2013/10/russell-brand-on-revolution.
2. Quoted in Hoffman, B. G. *American Icon: Alan Mulally and the Fight to Save Ford Motor Company.* New York: Crown, 2012, p. 126.

Chapter 1

1. Morran, C. "JCPenney Ends Ron Johnson Experiment, Sends CEO Packing." *Consumerist*, Apr. 8, 2013. http://consumerist.com/2013/04/08/jcpenney-ends-ron-johnson-experiment-sends-ceo-packing/.
2. Macke, J. "Ron Johnson's JCPenney: Anatomy of a Retail Failure." *Breakout* (blog), Yahoo Finance, Apr. 9, 2013. http://finance.yahoo.com/blogs/breakout/ron-johnson-jcpenney-anatomy-retail-failure-114635276.html.
3. Heisler, Y. "Former Apple Retail Guru Ron Johnson Shown the Door at JC Penney." *iOnApple* (blog), *Network World*, Apr. 9, 2013. http://www.networkworld.com/community/blog/former-apple-retail-guru-ron-johnson-shown-door-jc-penney.
4. Phillips, C. B., quoted in Denning, S. "J.C.Penney: Was Ron Johnson's Strategy Wrong?" *Forbes*, Apr. 9, 2013. http://www.forbes.com/sites/stevedenning/2013/04/09/j-c-penney-was-ron-johnsons-strategy-wrong/.
5. Quoted in Tuttle, B. "The 5 Big Mistakes That Led to Ron Johnson's Ouster at JC Penney." *Time*, Apr. 9, 2013. http://business.time.com/2013/04/09/the-5-big-mistakes-that-led-to-ron-johnsons-ouster-at-jc-penney/.
6. Ibid.
7. Bhasin, K. "Ron Johnson's Desperate Broadcasts to J.C. Penney Workers Fell Flat as Company Faltered." May 28, 2013. http://www.huffingtonpost.com/2013/05/28/ron-johnson-broadcasts_n_3348431.html.
8. Gerstner, L. *Who Says Elephants Can't Dance? Leading a Great Enterprise Through Dramatic Change.* New York: HarperBusiness, 2003, p. 16.

9. Morris, B. "He's Smart. He's Not Nice. He's Saving Big Blue." *Fortune*, Apr. 14, 1997. http://money.cnn.com/magazines/fortune/fortune_archive/1997/04/14/224974/index.htm.

10. Gerstner, *Who Says*, p. 68.

11. Ibid., p. 72.

12. Ibid., p. 182.

13. Bolman, L. G., and Deal, T. E. *The Wizard and the Warrior: Leading with Passion and Power*. San Francisco: Jossey-Bass, 2005, p. 180.

14. Ibid., p. 182.

15. Ibid., p. 183.

16. Barbaro, M. "Home Depot to Investors: Mea Culpa." *New York Times*, May 23, 2007, p. C1. http://www.nytimes.com/2007/05/23/business/23depot.html.

17. Goran Carstedt, quoted in Hampden-Turner, C. *Creating Corporate Culture: From Discord to Harmony*. Reading, Mass.: Addison-Wesley, 1992, p. 167. Carstedt led the turnaround of Volvo's French division in the 1980s.

18. Simon, H. A., and Chase, W. G. "Skill in Chess." *American Scientist*, 1973, *61*, 394–403.

19. Shermer, M. *The Believing Brain: From Ghosts and Gods to Politics and Conspiracies—How We Construct Beliefs and Reinforce Them as Truths*. New York: St. Martin's Griffin, 2012, p. 5.

20. Gladwell, M. *Blink: The Power of Thinking Without Thinking*. New York: Little, Brown, 2005.

21. Rocco, M. "Ten of the Worst CEOs Ever," accessed Feb. 16, 2014, http://www.foxbusiness.com/business-leaders/slideshow/2012/11/20/ten-worst-ceos/#slide=1. Portfolio.com (now *Upstart Business Journal*) asked a panel of professors at top business schools to rate the worst CEOs of all time: "Portfolio's Worst American CEOs of All Time," CNBC, accessed Feb. 16, 2014, http://www.cnbc.com/id/30502091/page/5.

22. McCall, M. W., Lombardo, M. M., and Morrison, A. M. *Lessons of Experience: How Successful Executives Develop on the Job*. New York: Free Press, 1988, p. 122.

23. Klein, A. "A Gate-Crasher's Change of Heart." *Breaking News Blog, Washington Post*, July 13, 2007. http://www.washingtonpost.com/wp-dyn/content/article/2007/07/12/AR2007071202356.html.

24. Ibid.

25. We first published these ideas in our book *Modern Approaches to Understanding and Managing Organizations*. San Francisco: Jossey-Bass, 1984.

26. Hubbard, D. W. *How to Measure Anything: Finding the Value of Intangibles in Business*. Hoboken, NJ: Wiley, 2010, p. 35.

27. Blanchard, K., and Barrett, C. *Lead with LUV: A Different Way to Create Real Success*. Upper Saddle River, NJ: FT Press, 2010, p. 7.

28. Pfeffer, J. *Power: Why Some People Have It and Others Don't*. New York: Harper Business, 2010, p. 5.
29. Logan, D., King, J., and Fischer-Wright, H. *Tribal Leadership: Leveraging Natural Groups to Build a Thriving Organization*. New York: HarperBusiness, 2011, p. 4.
30. Studies linking reframing to leadership effectiveness include Bensimon, E. M. "The Meaning of 'Good Presidential Leadership': A Frame Analysis." *Review of Higher Education*, 1989, *12*, 107–123; Bensimon, E. M. "Viewing the Presidency: Perceptual Congruence Between Presidents and Leaders on Their Campuses." *Leadership Quarterly*, 1990, *1*, 71–90; Dunford, R. W., and Palmer, I. C. "Claims About Frames: Practitioners' Assessment of the Utility of Reframing." *Journal of Management Education*, 1995, *19*, 96–105; Wimpelberg, R. K. "Managerial Images and School Effectiveness." *Administrators' Notebook*, 1987, *32*, 1–4.

Chapter 2

1. Niemann, G. *Big Brown: The Untold Story of UPS*. San Francisco: Jossey-Bass: 2007, p. 189.
2. Ibid., p. 8.
3. Galbraith, J. R. *Designing Organizations: An Executive Briefing on Strategy, Structure, and Process*. San Francisco: Jossey-Bass, 2001.
4. Love, J. F. *McDonald's: Behind the Arches*. New York: Bantam Books, 1986.
5. Chandler, A. D., Jr. *Strategy and Market Structure*. Cambridge, Mass.: Harvard University Press, 1962, p. 13.
6. Broder, J. M., and Schmitt, E. "U.S. Attacks on Holdouts Dealt Iraqis Final Blow." *New York Times*, Apr. 13, 2003, p. B1.
7. Drucker, P. F. "Peter Drucker's 1990s: The Futures That Have Already Happened." *Economist*, Oct. 21, 1989, p. 20.
8. This case is loosely adapted from Anne Donnellon and Dun Gifford Jr., "Campbell and Bailyn's Boston Office: Managing the Reorganization." Case study. Prod. no.: 2182-PDF-ENG. Boston: Harvard Business Publishing, Apr. 11, 2008.

Chapter 3

1. One of the best accounts of this widely covered story is Franklin, J. *33 Men*. New York: Putnam, 2011.
2. Ibid., p. 96.
3. Keidel, R. W. "Baseball, Football and Basketball: Models for Business." *Organizational Dynamics*, 1984 (Winter), p. 8.
4. Quoted in Keidel, "Baseball," pp. 14–15.

5. Ibid., p. 9.
6. Ibid., p. 15.
7. Ibid., p. 4.
8. Lubans, J. "More Than a Game." Working draft, Mar. 20, 2001. http://www .lubans.org/morethanagame.html.
9. Cohen, S. G., and Ledford, G. E., Jr. "The Effectiveness of Self-Managing Teams: A Quasi-Experiment." *Human Relations*, 1994, *47*, 13–43; Emery, C. R., and Fredendall, L. D. "The Effect of Teams on Firm Profitability and Customer Satisfaction." *Journal of Service Research*, 2002, *4*, 217–229.

Chapter 4

1. Davidson, A. "A Ready-to-Assemble Business Plan." *New York Times Magazine*, Jan. 5, 2014, pp. 12–13. http://www.nytimes.com/2014/01/05/ magazine/thinking-outside-the-big-box.html?_r=0.
2. Harnish, V., and the Editors of Fortune (eds.). *The Greatest Business Decisions of All Time*. New York: Fortune Books, 2012, pp. 200–201.
3. Ibid.
4. "James Sinegal, Costco." *Bloomberg Businessweek*, Sept. 22, 2002. http://www .businessweek.com/stories/2002-09-22/james-sinegal-costco.
5. McGregor, D. *The Human Side of Enterprise*. New York: McGraw-Hill, 1960.
6. Quoted in Bergman, L., Rummel, D., and MacIntyre, L. "A Dangerous Business." *Frontline*, 2003. www.pbs.org/wgbh/pages/frontline/shows/workplace/ mcwane/two.html; transcript at http://www.pbs.org/wgbh/pages/frontline/ shows/workplace/etc/script.html.
7. Semler, R. *Maverick: The Success Story Behind the World's Most Unusual Workplace*. New York: Warner Books, 1993, p. 67.
8. Killian, K., Perez, F., and Siehl, C. *Ricardo Semler and Semco S. A.* Phoenix: Thunderbird, 1998, p. 2.
9. Semler, R. *The Seven-Day Weekend: Changing the Way Work Works*. New York: Penguin, 2004, p. 78.
10. Pfeffer, J. "The Men's Wearhouse: Success in a Declining Industry." Case HR-5. Stanford, Calif.: Stanford Graduate School of Business, 1997.
11. Lee, L. "Spiffing Up Men's Wearhouse." *Bloomberg Businessweek*, Nov. 1, 2004. http://www.businessweek.com/magazine/content/04_44/b3906112 .htm.
12. "100 Best Companies to Work For." *Fortune*, 2013. http://money.cnn.com/ magazines/fortune/best-companies/2013/list/?iid=bc_sp_full.
13. Smith, A. "Men's Wearhouse: Why We Fired Zimmer." CNNMoney, June 25, 2013. http://money.cnn.com/2013/06/25/news/companies/zimmer-mens-wearhouse /index.html.

Chapter 5

1. Argyris, C. "Skilled Incompetence." *Harvard Business Review*, Sept. 1986. Available at https://cb.hbsp.harvard.edu/cbmp/search?term=argyris%2520sk illed%2520incompetence&navigation=0.
2. National Transportation Safety Board. "Aviation Accident Report: World Airways, Inc. DC-8-63F-N802WA, King Cove, Alaska, September 8, 1973." Washington, D.C.: National Transportation Safety Board, 1974. http://library online.erau.edu/online-full-text/ntsb/aircraft-accident-reports/AAR74-06.pdf.
3. Gregor, J. *Group Chairman's Factual Report of Investigation*. Washington, D.C.: National Transportation Safety Board, 2013. http://dms.ntsb.gov/ public%2F55000–55499%2F55433%2F544904.pdf.

Chapter 6

1. Morris, B. "The Accidental CEO," CNNMoney, June 23, 2003, http://money .cnn.com/magazines/fortune/fortune_archive/2003/06/23/344603/index.htm.
2. Morris, B. "She Was Never Groomed to Be the Boss. But Anne Mulcahy Is Bringing Xerox Back from the Dead." *Fortune*, June 23, 2003. http://money .cnn.com/magazines/fortune/fortune_archive/2003/06/23/344603.
3. Bianco, A., and Moore, P. L. "Xerox: The Downfall: The Inside Story of the Management Fiasco at Xerox," *Bloomberg Businessweek*, Mar. 5, 2001, http:// www.businessweek.com/2001/01_10/b3722001.htm.
4. A number of authors have developed this idea, including Kanter, R. M. *The Change Masters: Innovations for Productivity in the American Corporation*. New York: Simon & Schuster, 1983; Kotter, J. P. *The Leadership Factor*. New York: Free Press, 1988; Pfeffer, J. *Politics and Influence in Organizations*. Boston: Harvard Business School Press, 1992; Smith, H. *The Power Game*. New York: Random House, 1988.
5. Authors who have discussed political mapping include Bolman, L. G., and Deal, T. E. *Reframing Organizations: Artistry, Choice, and Leadership*, 4th ed. San Francisco: Jossey-Bass, 2008; Pfeffer, *Managing with Power: Politics and Influence in Organizations*. Boston: Harvard Business School Press, 1994; Pichault, F. *Ressources humaines et changement stratégique: Vers un management politique*. [Human resources and strategic change: Toward a political approach to management]. Brussels, Belgium: DeBoeck, 1993.
6. This idea is discussed in Bolman, L. G., and Deal, T. E. *The Wizard and the Warrior: Leading with Passion and Power*. San Francisco: Jossey-Bass, 2006; Kanter, *Change Masters*; Kotter, J. P. *Power and Influence: Beyond Formal Authority*. New York: Free Press 1985; Kotter, *Leadership Factor*; Pfeffer, *Managing with Power*; Smith, *Power Game*.
7. Among the many discussions of bargaining, see Bolman and Deal, *Reframing Organizations*; Kolb, D., and Williams, J. *Everyday Negotiation*. San Francisco:

Jossey-Bass, 2003; Fisher, R., and Ury, W. *Getting to Yes*. Boston: Houghton-Mifflin, 1981; Shell, G. R. *Bargaining for Advantage: Negotiation Strategies for Reasonable People*, 2nd ed. New York: Penguin, 2006.

8. Bennis, W. *Why Leaders Can't Lead: The Unconscious Conspiracy Continues*. San Francisco: Jossey-Bass, 1989, p. 20.

9. Kanter, *Change Masters*, p. 218.

10. Matthews, C. *Hardball*. New York: Free Press, 1999, p. 113.

11. Ibid., p. 114.

12. Kanter, *Change Masters*, p. 223.

13. Morris, "Accidental CEO."

14. Fisher and Ury, *Getting to Yes*.

15. Ibid., p. 39.

16. Morris, "Accidental CEO."

17. George, B. *True North*. San Francisco: Jossey-Bass, 2007, p. 174.

18. Accounts of Cooper's story include Cooper, C. *Extraordinary Circumstances: The Journey of a Corporate Whistleblower*. Hoboken, NJ: Wiley, 2008; Ripley, A. "The Night Detective." *Time*, Dec. 22, 2002. http://www.time.com/time/magazine/article/0,9171,1003990,00.html; Kaplan, R. S., and Kiron, D. "Accounting Fraud at WorldCom." Case study. Prod. no.: 104071-PDF-ENG. Boston: Harvard Business School, Apr. 29, 2004. (Rev. Sept. 2007.)

Chapter 7

1. Heffron, F. *Organization Theory and Public Organizations: The Political Connection*. Upper Saddle River, NJ: Prentice Hall, 1989, p. 185.

2. Isaacson, W. *Steve Jobs*. New York: Simon & Schuster, 2011.

3. Reingold, J. "Bob Iger: Disney's Fun King." *Fortune*, May 12, 2012, pp. 166–174. http://management.fortune.cnn.com/2012/05/09/500-disney-iger/.

4. Isaacson, *Steve Jobs*, p. 436.

5. Reingold, "Fun King," p. 169.

6. Isaacson, *Steve Jobs*, p. 438.

7. Ibid., p. 439.

8. Heifetz, R. A., and Linsky, M. *Leadership on the Line: Staying Alive Through the Dangers of Leading*. Boston: Harvard Business School Press, 2002, p. 12.

9. Kipling, R. "If." Accessed Feb. 16, 2014, from http://www.everypoet.com/archive/poetry/Rudyard_Kipling/kipling_if.htm.

10. Klein, M. *The Change Makers: From Carnegie to Gates, How the Great Entrepreneurs Transformed Ideas into Industries*. New York: Time Books, 2003.

11. Brands, H. W. *Masters of Enterprise: Giants of American Business from John Jacob Astor and J. P. Morgan to Bill Gates and Oprah Winfrey*. New York: Free Press, 1999.

12. Bolman, L. G., and Deal, T. E. *The Wizard and the Warrior: Leading with Passion and Power*. San Francisco: Jossey-Bass, 2006.
13. Ortega, B. *In Sam We Trust: The Untold Story of Sam Walton and Wal-Mart, the World's Most Powerful Retailer*. Pittsburgh: Three Rivers Press, 1998.

Chapter 8
1. "Our Tribal Culture," WD-40 Company, http://www.wd40company.com/about/careers/our-tribal-culture/.
2. "Our Passion," WD-40 Company, http://www.wd40company.com/about/careers/our-passion/.
3. "Our Core Values" [video], WD-40 Company, http://www.wd40company.com/about/careers/our-tribal-culture/.
4. Ibid.
5. Schultz, H. *Onward: How Starbucks Fought for Its Life Without Losing Its Soul.* New York: Rodale, 2011, p. 24.
6. Ibid., p. 25.
7. Ibid., p. 38.
8. Ibid., p. 3.
9. Ibid., p. 112.
10. Ibid.
11. Ibid., p. 131.
12. Ibid., p. 198.
13. Ibid., p. 200.
14. Ibid., pp. 203–204.
15. Ibid., p. 206.
16. Ibid., p. 13.
17. Ibid., p. 12.
18. Carlzon, J. *Moments of Truth*. New York: Ballinger, 1987.

Chapter 9
1. Leavitt, H. J., and Lipman-Blumen, J. *Hot Groups*. Oxford: Oxford University Press, 1999.
2. Isaacson, W. *Steve Jobs*. New York: Simon & Schuster, 2011, p. 144.
3. Pfarrer, C. *Seal Target Geronimo: The Inside Story of the Mission to Kill Osama bin Laden*. New York: Macmillan, 2011, p. 29.
4. Ibid.
5. Schlesinger, L., Eccles, R., and Gabarro, J. *Managerial Behavior in Organizations*. New York: McGraw-Hill, 1983, p. 173.
6. Kidder, T. *The Soul of a New Machine*. New York: Little, Brown, 1981.
7. Ibid., p. 179.
8. Ibid., p. 109.

9. Ibid., p. 119.

10. Ibid., p. 116.

11. Ibid., p. 179.

12. Ibid., p. 191.

13. Ibid., p. 66.

14. Ibid., p. 63.

15. Ibid., p. 75.

16. Ibid., p. 60.

17. Ibid., p. 50.

18. Ibid., p. 44.

19. Ibid., p. 132.

20. Ibid., p. 250.

21. Ibid., p. 105.

22. Ibid., pp. 109–110.

23. Vaill, P. "The Purposing of High-Performance Systems." *Organizational Dynamics*, Autumn 1982, pp. 23–39.

24. Bennis, W. G. "The Secrets of Great Groups." *Leader to Leader*, Winter 1997, no. 3. This article can be accessed at http://www.leadershipasheville.org/blog/wp-content/uploads/2012/10/Bennis-The-Secrets-of-Great-Groups.pdf.

Chapter 10

1. Gallos, J. V., Ramsey, V. J., and Associates. *Teaching Diversity: Listening to the Soul, Speaking from the Heart.* San Francisco: Jossey-Bass, 1997, p. 216.

Chapter 11

1. Helft, M. "Mark Zuckerberg's Most Valuable Friend." *New York Times*, Oct. 2, 2010. http://www.nytimes.com/2010/10/03/business/03face.html?_r=0.

2. Helft, M. "Sheryl Sandberg: The Real Story." *Fortune*, Oct. 28, 2013, pp. 123–130. http://money.cnn.com/2013/10/10/leadership/sheryl-sandberg-mpw.pr.fortune/.

3. Rivlin, G. "A Retail Revolution Turns 10." *New York Times*, July 10, 2005. http://www.nytimes.com/2005/07/10/business/yourmoney/10amazon.html?_r=0.

4. Anders, G. "Jeff Bezos Gets It." *Forbes*, Apr. 23, 2012, pp. 76–86. http://www.forbes.com/sites/georgeanders/2012/04/04/inside-amazon/.

5. Anders, "Jeff Bezos Gets It," p. 77.

6. Ibid., p. 77.

7. Stone, B. *The Everything Store: Jeff Bezos and the Age of Amazon.* New York: Little, Brown, 2013, p. 177.

8. Anders, "Jeff Bezos Gets It," p. 77.

9. We have relied on several sources for the Zappos story. A good place to start is Tony Hsieh's book, *Delivering Happiness: A Path to Profits, Passion, and*

Purpose. New York: Business Plus, 2010. Other sources include Schoenmann, J. "What's Behind Tony Hsieh's Unrelenting Drive to Remake Downtown Las Vegas?" *Las Vegas Sun,* Apr. 20, 2012; Rich, M. "Why Is This Man Smiling?" *New York Times,* Apr. 8, 2011. http://www.nytimes.com/2011/04/10/fashion/10HSEIH.html?pagewanted=all; Frei, F. X., Ely, R. J., and Winig, L. "Zappos.com 2009: Clothing, Customer Service, and Company Culture." Case study. Prod. 610015-PDF-ENG. Boston: Harvard Business School, Oct. 20, 2009; Hsieh, T. "CEO Letter." 2009. http://blogs.zappos.com/ceoletter.

10. Weisul, K. "A Shine on Their Shoes: Zappos.com's Blue-Ribbon Customer Service Is Winning Market Share." *Bloomberg Businessweek,* Dec. 5, 2005. http://www.businessweek.com/magazine/content/05_49/b3962118.htm.

11. "Zappos Family Music Video," YouTube, Aug. 30, 2010, http://www.youtube.com/watch?v=4gHlEBU_NSg.

12. Brown, V. "The Importance of a Company's 'Culture.'" Interview with Tony Hsieh. Bigthink.com, June 30, 2010. http://bigthink.com/ideas/20672.

13. Pestrak, D. *Playing with the Big Boys.* New York: Sun, 2001, p. 167.

14. McGirt, E. "Fresh Copy: How Ursula Burns Reinvented Xerox." *Fast Company,* Nov. 19, 2011. http://www.fastcompany.com/magazine/161/ursula-burns-xerox.

15. Ibid.

16. Pestrak, *Playing,* p. 174.

17. Isaacson, W. *Steve Jobs.* New York: Simon & Schuster, 2011, p. 196.

18. Ibid., p. 197.

19. Jobs, S. Commencement Address at Stanford University, June 2005. http://news.stanford.edu/news/2005/june15/jobs-061505.html.

20. Isaacson, W. *Steve Jobs.* New York: Simon & Schuster, 2011, p. 474.

21. A video of Jobs at the iPhone launch event can be found at "Steve Jobs Introduces iPhone in 2007," YouTube, http://www.youtube.com/watch?v=MnrJzXM7a6o.

22. Lashinsky, A. "Inside Apple." *Fortune,* May 23, 2011, pp. 126–134.

23. Lashinsky, A. "How Apple Works: Inside the World's Biggest Startup." *Fortune,* Aug. 25, 2011. http://tech.fortune.cnn.com/2011/08/25/how-apple-works-inside-the-worlds-biggest-startup/. (This article appeared in the May 23, 2011, issue of *Fortune* magazine.)

24. Lashinsky, "Inside Apple," p. 128.

25. Lashinsky, "How Apple Works."

Chapter 12

1. Machiavelli, N. *The Prince.* G. Bull (ed.). New York: Penguin Classics, 1961, p. 27. (Originally published 1514.)

2. Cohen, M., and March, J. G. *Leadership and Ambiguity.* New York: McGraw-Hill, 1974, p. 203.

3. Edelman, M. J. *The Symbolic Uses of Politics*. Madison: University of Wisconsin Press, 1977, p. 73.

4. Hindo, B. "At 3M, a Struggle Between Efficiency and Creativity." *Bloomberg Businessweek*, June 10, 2007, http://www.businessweek.com/stories/2007-06-10/at-3m-a-struggle-between-efficiency-and-creativity.

5. Ibid.

6. Conlin, M., and Greene, J. "How to Make a Microserf Smile." *Bloomberg Businessweek*, Sept. 9, 2007. http://www.businessweek.com/stories/2007-09-09/how-to-make-a-microserf-smile.

7. "2011 World's Best Multinational Workplaces." Great Place to Work. http://www.greatplacetowork.com/best-companies/worlds-best-multinationals/the-list/1509-2011.

8. Hoffman, B. G. *American Icon: Alan Mulally and the Fight to Save Ford Motor Company*. New York: Crown, 2012, pp. 136–137.

9. Ibid., p. 88.

10. Ibid., p. 142.

11. Ibid., p. 106.

12. Ibid., p. 109.

13. Ibid., pp. 103–104.

14. Ibid., p. 104.

15. Ibid., pp. 247–248.

16. Ibid., pp. 133–134. The ad is pictured among the photographs on pp. 214 and 215.

17. Ibid., pp. 134–135.

Chapter 13

1. Thomas, K. "After Recalls and Missteps, J.&J.'s New Chief Confronts Critical Challenges." *New York Times*, Apr. 25, 2012. http://www.nytimes.com/2012/04/26/business/big-challenges-ahead-for-johnsons-new-chief.html?_r=0.

2. Kimes, M. "Johnson & Johnson CEO Bill Weldon's Painful Year." CNNMoney, Sept. 7, 2010. http://money.cnn.com/2010/09/06/news/companies/J_and_J_Bill_Weldon_Bad_Year.fortune/.

3. "Patients Versus Profits at Johnson & Johnson: Has the Company Lost Its Way?" *Knowledge@Wharton*, Feb. 15, 2012. http://knowledge.wharton.upenn.edu/article/patients-versus-profits-at-johnson-johnson-has-the-company-lost-its-way/.

4. George, B., and Van de Ven, A. "Medtronic's Chairman William George on How Mission-Driven Companies Create Long-Term Shareholder Value." *Academy of Management Executive*, 2001, *15*(4), pp. 39–47.

5. Bolman, L. G., and Deal, T. E. *Leading with Soul: An Uncommon Journey of Spirit*. San Francisco: Jossey-Bass, 2011, p. 122.

6. Ibid., pp. 128–129.

7. Levering, R., and Moskowitz, M. *The 100 Best Companies to Work For in America*. New York: Plume, 1993.

8. George, B. *True North*. San Francisco: Jossey-Bass, 2007.

9. Ewen, B. "Persistence Is the Difference for Marilyn Carlson Nelson, Carlson Cos." Leader." *Upsizemag.com*, 2009. http://www.upsizemag.com/back-page/marilyn-carlson-nelson.

10. Solomon, R. C. *Ethics and Excellence: Cooperation and Integrity in Business*. Oxford: Oxford University Press, 1993, p. 231.

11. Robinson, A. G., and Schroeder, D. M. *The Idea-Driven Organization*. San Francisco: Berrett-Koehler, 2014.

12. O'Neill, T. P. "Frenemies: A Love Story." *Campaign Stops* (blog), *New York Times*, Oct. 5, 2013. http://campaignstops.blogs.nytimes.com/2012/10/05/frenemies-a-love-story/.

13. Neuman, J. "Former President Reagan Dies at 93." *Los Angeles Times*, June 6, 2004. p. 1. http://www.latimes.com/news/obituaries/la-reagan,0,2289200.story#axzz2uNVjUa6t.

14. Gallos, J. V., Ramsey, V. J., and Associates. *Teaching Diversity: Listening to the Soul, Speaking from the Heart*. San Francisco: Jossey-Bass, 1997.

15. Cox, T., Jr. *Cultural Diversity in Organizations: Theory, Research, and Practice*. San Francisco: Berrett-Koehler, 1994; Gallos, Ramsey, and Associates, *Teaching Diversity*; Morrison, A. M. *The New Leaders: Guidelines on Leadership Diversity in America*. San Francisco: Jossey-Bass, 1992.

16. Kidder, T. *The Soul of a New Machine*. New York: Little, Brown, 1989, p. 313.

17. Gurowitz, M. "James E. Burke, 1925–2012," *Kilmer House: The Story of Johnson and Johnson and Its People* (blog), Oct. 1, 2012. http://www.kilmerhouse.com/2012/10/james-e-burke-1925-2012/.

18. Griffin, E. *The Reflective Executive: A Spirituality of Business and Enterprise*. New York: Crossroads, 1993, p. 178.

19. De Pree, M. *Leadership Is an Art*. New York: Dell, 1989, p. 69.

Chapter 14

1. Gottschall, J. *The Storytelling Animal: How Stories Make Us Human*. New York: Mariner, 2013.

2. Thau, B. "Ron Johnson Speaks, Calls Reports on His J.C. Penney Tenure 'Largely Inaccurate and Surprisingly Uninformed.'" *Forbes*, Oct. 29, 2013. http://www.forbes.com/sites/barbarathau/2013/10/29/an-open-letter-to-ex-j-c-penney-ceo-ron-johnson-who-calls-reports-on-his-tenure-surprisingly-uninformed-when-youre-ready-can-we-talk/.

3. Taylor, A., III. "Fixing Up Ford." *Fortune*, May 12, 2009. http://money.cnn .com/2009/05/11/news/companies/mulally_ford.fortune/index.htm.
4. Bolman, L. G., and Deal, T. E. *The Wizard and the Warrior: Leading with Passion and Power*. San Francisco: Jossey-Bass, 2006, p. 180.
5. Prusak, L., Groh, K., Denning, S., and Seely Brown, J. *Storytelling in Organizations*. Burlington, Mass.: Elsevier, 2004, p. 4.

THE AUTHORS

Lee G. Bolman holds the Marion Block Missouri Chair in Leadership at the Bloch School of Management, University of Missouri–Kansas City. He received a BA (1962) in history and a PhD (1968) in administrative sciences, both from Yale University. Bolman's interests lie at the intersection of leadership and organizations, and he has published numerous articles, chapters, and cases. He is coauthor of *Reframing Academic Leadership* (with Joan V. Gallos, 2011). Bolman has been a consultant to corporations, public agencies, universities, and public schools in the United States, Asia, Europe, and Latin America. For twenty years, he taught at the Harvard Graduate School of Education, where he also chaired the Institute for Educational Administration and the School Leadership Academy. He has been director and board chair of the Organizational Behavior Teaching Society and director of the National Training Laboratories.

Bolman lives in Brookline, Massachusetts, with his wife, Joan Gallos, and a spirited Theory Y cockapoo, Douglas McGregor.

Terrence E. Deal has served on the faculties of Stanford, Harvard, Vanderbilt, and the University of Southern California. He received his BA (1961) from the University of La Verne (ULV), his MA (1966) from California State University at Los Angeles, and his PhD (1972) in sociology and administration from Stanford University. Deal has been a police officer, public school teacher, high school principal, district administrator, and university professor.

His primary research interests are in organizations, symbolism, and change. He is the author or coauthor of twenty-seven books, including the best seller *Corporate Cultures* (with Allan A. Kennedy, 1982) and

Shaping School Culture (with Kent D. Peterson, 1999). He has published many articles on organizations, change, and leadership. He is a consultant to business, health care, military, educational, and religious organizations domestically and in Europe, Scandinavia, the Middle East, Canada, South America, Japan, and Southeast Asia. He is the founder of ULV's Deal Leadership Institute.

Deal lives in San Luis Obispo's Edna Valley, California, with his wife, Sandy. He is semiretired from university life. Along with writing, his current avocation is winemaking as a member of the Edna Ranch Vintner's Guild.

Bolman and Deal first met in 1976 when they were assigned to coteach a course on organization at Harvard University. Trained in different disciplines on opposite coasts, they disagreed on almost everything. It was the beginning of a challenging but very productive partnership. They have written a number of other books together, including *Reframing Organizations: Artistry, Choice, and Leadership*, and *Leading with Soul: An Uncommon Journey of Spirit*. Their books have been translated into multiple languages for readers in Asia, Europe, and Latin America.

For five years, Bolman and Deal also codirected the National Center for Educational Leadership, a research consortium of Harvard, Vanderbilt, and the University of Chicago.

The authors appreciate hearing from readers and welcome comments, questions, suggestions, or accounts of experiences that bear on the ideas in the book. Stories of success, failure, or puzzlement are all welcome. Readers can contact the authors at the following addresses:

Lee Bolman
7 Hawes Street
Brookline, MA 02446
lee@bolman.com

Terry Deal
6625 Via Piedra
San Luis, Obispo CA 93401
sucha@surfnetusa.com

INDEX

Page references followed by *fig* indicate an illustrated figure; followed by *e* indicate an exhibit.

Basketball team structure, 46–47

Beatles' Shea Stadium concert (New York), 111

Beliefs: as element of leader's worldview, 190–191; self-images based on virtues and, 68; stories that give flesh to shared values and, 185. *See also* Cultural symbols and values

Bennis, Warren, 81, 127

Bezos, Jeff: as Amazon founder, 23; concepts, categories, and beliefs included in worldview of, 189; lack of human resource leadership displayed by, 147*fig*, 156; leadership configuration used by, 147*fig*, 149; metrics maestro leadership image of, 146–149, 157

bin Laden, Osama, 45, 119, 120

Blink (Gladwell), 11

Blodgett, Lynn, 153

Bloomberg Businessweek, 80

Boeing, 47, 161, 166, 168, 188

Bono, 113

Brand, Russell, 1

Brummel, Lisa, 162–163

Buckley, George, 161–162

Buffett, Warren, 93

Bureaucracy, 24

Burke, James E., 175, 176, 184–185

Burns, Ursula: leadership configuration of, 152*fig*; leadership image as an authentic engineer, 151–153; successful leadership of Xerox by, 23, 84, 151–153

C

Camp David Accords (1978), 85–86

Caring and love (human resource frame), 178*e*, 180–181

Carlson Companies, 180–181

Carlzon, Jan, 117

Ceremonies. *See* Rituals and ceremonies

Cézanne, Paul, 14

Change: leadership challenges related to, 159; limits of leadership in managing, 159–160

Change management: carriers versus catalysts approach to, 160–163;

comparing skidding automobile to command-and-control capabilities of college presidents, 160; faith in leaders' abilities to create successful, 159–160; four-frame model used for, 163–172; Lisa Brummel's successful approach at Microsoft, 162–163; rooted in a shared understanding of challenges, 162

Change management frames: analysis of Ford Motor's resurrection using the, 165–172; human resource, 164*e*–165; political, 164*e*–165; structural, 164*e*–165; symbolic, 164*e*–165

Chess masters, 11

Chilean miner rescue (2010): comparing leadership dynamics of *Lord of the Flies* and the, 41–43; group dynamics during the, 39–41

Chrysler: Bob Nardelli's failure as CEO of, 12–13; U.S. government bailout of, 171, 191

Cluelessness: of Bob Nardelli as CEO of Home Depot, 9–10, 12, 13, 162; as failure of "common sense," 10; of Ron Johnson as CEO of JCPenney, 190

Coalition building skills, 83–85

Coca-Cola, 107

Cohen, M., 160

"The Commoditization of the Starbucks Experience" memo (Schultz), 109

Conflict: as inevitable in all social interactions, 91; Lois Payne case example of handling, 100–102; negotiation and bargaining skills to manage, 85–87; peacemaker approach to, 91, 93–97, 101; personal and emotional overtones of, 94; political dealings and role of, 89; technical and adaptive problems that cause, 94–95; warrior approach to, 91–94, 97–100, 101. *See also* Political dynamics

Contextual factors (or structural contingencies): core process, 29*e*–30; information technology, 29*e*, 30–31; nature of the workforce, 29*e*, 31; size and age, 28–29*e*; strategy and goals, 29*e*, 30

Cook, Tim, 156
Cooper, Cynthia, 87–88
Costco: enlightened employee management at, 51, 52; Jim Sinegal's CEO position at, 4, 52
Couric, Katie, 63–64
"Court sense," 12
Cross, Irv, 46
Cultural symbols and values: danger of importing from one company to another, 161–162; examples of values that bond companies, 108; how symbolic leaders (Magicians) work with, 114–118; Starbucks's story on revival of, 108–115; stories that give flesh to shared, 185; of the WD-40 company, 107–108; Zappos employees trained using, 150–151. *See also* Beliefs; Virtues
Customer service: Amazon's focus on lowest priced and best, 147, 148–149; and decline of Home Depot, 10; reframing IBM's, 8; Zappos's extraordinary levels of, 108, 149–151, 157

D
Dallas Cowboys, 46
Dartmouth, 6
Data General. *See* Eagle Group (Data General)
Davidson, Adam, 51
Davis, Jack. *See* Davis-Martin case study
Davis-Martin case study: facing a serious leadership challenge, 131–132, 143; human resource scenario reframing response by the, 134–136; political scenario reframing response by the, 136–139; structural scenario reframing response by the, 132–134; symbolic scenario reframing response by the, 139–141
DC-8 airline flight crash, 70–72
de Castro, Edson, 122, 123
De Pree, Max, 185
Decision making: how fluid expertise facilitates, 12–13; for technical versus adaptive problems, 94–95; U.S. Army

commando team, 43–44. *See also* Leadership ethics
Defense of Marriage Act, 79
Delivering Happiness (Hsieh), 149
Digital Equipment Corporation, 6
Dilbert (cartoon strip), 53
Disney, Roy, 92, 93
Diversity. *See* Employee diversity
Dockers, 4
Duke University: women's basketball team, 47

E
Eagle Group (Data General): contribution of informal cultural players to the, 126–127; examining the success of the, 120–121; example approach used by members of the, 123; humor and play as part of the work processes, 124–125; leadership diversity used as competitive advantage by, 122–123; mushroom management used by the, 121; ritual and ceremony used by the, 125–126; "signing up" ritual of the, 121–122; specialized language used within the, 123–124; stories and group lore used by the, 124
Eagleman, David, 11
Eastman, George, 97
Egypt, and Camp David Accords (1978), 85–86
Eisner, Michael, 92–93, 94, 101, 156
Ellen and Don's story, 65–67, 73–76
Ellison, Larry, 97
Emotions: defusing, 96–97; human resource frame's focus on caring and love, 178e, 180–181; listening and inquiring to understand other people's, 95
Employee diversity: Men's Wearhouse's commitment to, 61; Semco's programs to increase, 58–59
Employee empowerment: as buzzword versus genuine, 58; of Carlson Companies, 181; Men's Wearhouse approach to, 61; Semco's approach to, 58

leadership and management approach of the, 51–62; Men's Wearhouse employee management using the, 59–62; Olivia Martin case study using the human resource scenario, 134–136; overcoming interpersonal blindness through the, 63–76; people-friendly principles of the, 49, 55e; reframing ethical leadership using the family metaphor of the, 178e, 180–181; Semco turnaround using the, 54–59; Steve Jobs's rare display of the, 156. *See also* Four-frame model

Humor, and play, 124–125

I

IBM: Charlie Chaplin commercials and THINK slogan of, 6; cultural values, language, and beliefs of, 7, 8; financial decline facing, 5–6; Lou Gerstner's stories to illuminate history and future of, 193; Lou Gerstner's successful reengineering of, 5–8, 23, 170, 192–193; reframing customer service at, 8

The Idea-Driven Organization (Robinson and Schroeder), 182

Iger, Bob: appointed to replace Michael Eisner, 93; as a peacemaker, 91, 93–94

Ikea (Brooklyn store), 51

Il Giornale, 114

Illanes, Juan, 39

Immelt, Jeff, 161

Incognito (Eagleman), 11

Information technology: as contextual factor or structural contingency, 29e; role of in Iraq invasion (2003), 30–31

Inquiry. *See* Advocacy and inquiry skills

Interpersonal blindness: as common problem in business encounters, 64–65; conflict between virtuous self-image and self-interest resulting in, 68; Ellen and Don's story of, 65–67, 73–76; how increased self-awareness can prevent, 68–73; Lao-tzu's words on, 67–68; Sarah Palin's interview (2008) as example of, 63–64

Interpersonal feedback principles: 1: ask and you shall receive, 69; 2: say thank you, 69; 3: ask before giving, 69–70; 4: when asked, give your best, 70; 5: tell the truth, 70–73

iPhone, 154–156

iPod, 155, 156

Iraq invasion (2003), 30–31

Israel, and Camp David Accords (1978), 85–86

iTunes, 92

Ive, Jony, 156

Izod, 4

J

Jackson, Phil, 46

JCPenney: need for turnaround at, 3; Ron Johnson's failed vision for transforming, 3–5, 8, 9, 192; Wal-Mart's market challenge to, 99

Jobs, Steve: ability to recruit and rally his team, 99; battle between Michael Eisner and, 92–93, 94, 101, 156; Bob Iger's peacemaking with, 91, 93–94; epitomizing the warrior, 91–93, 97, 98; fired from Apple, 154; his band of "Pirates," 119; investment in Pixar by, 92–94, 154; iPhone launch publicity approach by, 154–156; lack of human resource leadership displayed by, 156; leadership configuration of, 155fig; as master of the symbolic frame, 154–156; NeXT failure of, 154; passion and commitment of, 98; showmanship of, 113; warrior artist leadership image of, 91–93, 153–156

Joe Fresh, 4

Johnson, Ron: comparison of Lou Gerstner and, 8; failed vision for transforming JCPenney, 3–5, 8, 157, 192; lack of self-awareness by, 190; poor thinking evidenced by, 9, 10; single-lens view of, 15

Johnson & Johnson (J&J): Burke's Credo Challenge meetings held at, 184–185; Burke's ethical response to the Tylenol crisis (1982), 175, 176; J&J Credo of, 175, 176; recent ethical scandals involving, 176, 185

JoJo's Ritz-Carlton adventure story, 117

Jungle metaphor (political frame): introduction to the, 16, 17, 19*e*; leader's power and justice contribution to the, 178*e*, 181–183; reframing ethical leadership using the, 178*e*, 181–183

Justice and power (political frame), 178*e*, 181–183

K

Kanter, Rosabeth, 83–84

Keidel, R. W., 46

Kelleher, Herb, 108

Kennedy, John F., 115

Kentucky Fried Chicken, 107

Kidder, Tracy, 120, 121, 184

King, Martin Luther, Jr., 14

Kramer, Michael, 4

Kroc, Ray, 25, 28–29

Kurosawa, Akira, 20

L

Lao-tzu, 67–68

Larsen, Ralph, 176

Lateral authority structure, 28

Lead with LUV: A Different Way to Create Real Success (families metaphor), 15, 17

Leader worldview: four key elements of a, 189–190; the leader's story created through their own, 190–193; as part of the leadership process, 188*fig*

Leader worldview elements: beliefs, 189–190; concepts and categories, 189; self-image, 190; values, 190

Leaders: carriers versus catalysts of change, 160–163; human resource frame used by, 15, 17, 19*e*, 49–76; interpersonal blindness by, 63–76; as Magicians, 107–118; often portrayed as change agents, 159–160; as Peacemakers, 91, 93–97, 101; political frame used by, 16, 17, 19*e*, 77, 79–87, 91–103; self-awareness of effective, 68–73; spiritual, 178*e*, 183–185; structural frame

used by, 16, 19*e*, 24–48; worldviews and frames for weaving their own stories, 129, 187–193; as Warriors, 91–93, 97–101, 153–156

Leadership: advocacy and inquiry skills of, 73*fig*–76; aligning team structure and task, 48; challenges related to managing change, 159–173; comparing *Lord of the Flies* and Chilean miners, 41–43; failed model in *Lord of the Flies* (Golding), 37–39, 41–43; interpersonal blindness issue of, 63–76; and saga of the trapped Chilean miners, 39–43; worldviews, frames, and stories of, 188*fig*–193. *See also* Structural leadership

Leadership ethics: four-frame model for reframing, 178*e*–185; human resource frame, family metaphor, and leader's love and caring, 178*e*, 180–181; Johnson & Johnson (J&J) Tylenol crisis response and, 175, 176; as making all the difference to organizations, 177–178; Medtronic led by Bill George's, 176–177, 178; political frame, jungle metaphor, and leader's power and justice, 178*fig*, 181–183; recent scandals related to, 175–176; structural frame, factory metaphor, and leader's authorship of excellence, 178*e*, 179; symbolic frame, temple metaphor, and leader's faith and significance, 178*e*, 183–185. *See also* Decision making

Leadership images: of Amazon's Jeff Bezos, 146–149, 157; of Apple's Steve Jobs, 153–156; overview of, 145–146; of Xerox's Ursula Burns, 151–153; of Zappos's Tony Hsieh, 149–151, 157. *See also* Four-frame model

Leadership kite configurations: Jeff Bezos's, 147*fig*; Steve Jobs's, 155*fig*; Tony Hsieh's, 150*fig*; Ursula Burns's, 152*fig*

Leadership Orientations Profile, 132, 146

Leadership practices: holistic and multiframe approach to change, 129, 159–173; knowing their leadership kite and their blind spots, 129, 145–157;

189–190; "The Commoditization of the Starbucks Experience" memo by, 109; concerns about the direction of Starbucks, 109–110; cultural revival at Starbucks led by, 108–115; effective change management by, 162; *Fortune* magazine's Businessperson of the Year award to, 113; *Il Giornale* founded by, 114; leadership summit convened by, 110–111; leading by example, 116; New Orleans extravaganza led by, 112–113, 117–118; purchase of chain of Starbucks stores by, 114–115; showmanship of, 113; on Starbucks as a "living legacy" to his father, 116. *See also* Starbucks

Schultz, Mark, 169

Scotch Tape, 161

Sculley, John, 99, 154

Seal Team Six's Red Squadron, 119–120, 127, 128

Seale, Rosemarie, 127

Sears, 99

Self-awareness: importance to leadership strengths and weaknesses, 190; ongoing learning for development of, 68; principles of interpersonal feedback to increase, 69–73; 360-degree feedback designed to increase, 68

Self-directed teams: of Chilean miners during rescue, 39–43; corporations capitalizing on benefits of, 47; difference between "leaderless" and, 47; leadership as critical to, 47; *Lord of the Flies* dystopian novel on, 37–39, 41–43, 47. *See also* Team structure

Self-image: of Alan Mulally, 191; conflict between self-interest and virtuous, 68; as an element of leader's worldview, 190; Lao-tzu's words on, 67–68

Semco: developing a philosophy and values at, 55–56; empowering employees of, 58; founding and early development of, 53; hiring and keeping the right people at, 56–57; ideas on human resource frame gained from story of, 59; investing in people at, 57–58; principles for leading people implemented at, 55e; promoting employee diversity at, 58–59; Ricardo Semler's human resource approach to turnaround at, 54–59; unorthodox philosophy of management at, 56

Semco programs: "Lost in Space," 57; "name your price" compensation experiment, 57; "open-book management," 58; "Rush Hour MBA," 57–58; "Semco Woman" project, 55e, 59

Semler, Curt, 53, 54

Semler, Ricardo: beliefs and values that influence his worldview, 189, 190; turning around Semco by investing in people, 54–59

Sepúlveda, Mario, 39–41, 42

Setting agendas, 81

Shanahan, Betty, 126

Significance and faith (symbolic frame), 178e, 183–185

Sinegal, Jim, 4, 52

"Situational awareness," 12

Situations: framing to match mental maps to, 13; learning to tell the truth about, 70–73; "rapid cognition" of, 11–12; reframing to shift frames when circumstances change, 13–14

Six Sigma, 10, 161, 163; "Black Belt," 161

"Skilled incompetence," 67

Skunk Works (Lockheed Martin), 119, 127, 128

Social architecture: contextual factors or structural contingencies, 28–31; elements of, 27–28; six work group options, 27–28; two common misconceptions of, 23–27; as the underpinning of successful leaders, 23. *See also* Organizations

Solomon, Robert C., 181

Sony, 156

Soul: dictionary definition of, 178; organization's spirit and, 176–178

The Soul of a New Machine (Kidder), 120

strategy using the, 164e–165; Olivia Martin case study using symbolic scenario, 139–141; reframing ethical leadership using the temple/theater metaphor of, 178e, 183–185; scripts and rituals used in the, 105, 117–118; shared cultural patterns of the, 107; Steve Jobs as a master of the, 154–156; strategies used by leaders in the, 114–118; temple/theater frame concepts, 16, 17–18, 19e; WD-40 example of cultural symbols, 107–108. *See also* Four-frame model

Symbolic leaders: developing and communicating a hopeful vision, 115–116; Howard Schultz as a, 108–115; interpreting experience, 115; leading by example, 116; respecting and using history, 114–115; rituals and ceremonies used by, 105, 117–118; storytelling by, 116–117

T

Target (company), 3, 192

Team structure: of baseball team, 44–45; of basketball team, 46–47; of football team, 45–46; leadership that aligns tasks and, 48; task and, 43–44; U.S. Army commando team's success due to fluid, 43–44. *See also* Self-directed teams

Teams: examining leadership dynamics of, 39–48; soulful, 119–128; task and structure in, 43–47; Warrior ability to recruit and rally, 99. *See also* Groups

Technical problems, 94–95

Temple/theater metaphor (symbolic frame): introduction to the, 16, 17–18, 19e; leader's faith and significance contribution to the, 178e, 183–185; reframing ethical leadership using the, 178e, 183–185

TGI Fridays, 180

Thinking. *See* Leadership thinking

360-degree feedback, 68

3M, 161–162, 166

Time magazine, 154–155

T. J. Watson Research Center, 5

Top-down policies, 24

Tournament of Roses Parade (2014), 79

Toy Story (film), 92

Toy Story III (film), 93

Trader Joe's, 51

"Treat 'em like dirt" management, 52, 53

Tribal Leadership: Leveraging Natural Groups to Build a Thriving Organization (temples and carnivals metaphor), 16, 17–18

Triscuit brand, 5

Troubled auditor case study, 87–88

Truman, Harry, 89

U

Ullman, Myron, 3, 5

United Automobile Workers (UAW), 167, 191

United Parcel Service (UPS): failure to keep up with 2013 holiday demand, 148; organizational structure of, 24; work groups organized around process and workflow, 28

University of Minnesota, 180

UNIX operating system, 6

Updike, John, 45

Ury, William L., 85–86

Urzúa, Luis, 39–41, 42

U.S. Army commando team, 43–44

U.S. Supreme Court Defense of Marriage Act decision, 79

V

Vaill, Peter, 127

Vanderbilt, Cornelius, 97

Venture Frogs, 149

Vertical authority structure, 28

Virtues: caring and love, 178e, 180–181; conflict between self-interest and, 68; excellence, 178e, 179; faith and significance, 178e, 183–185; justice and power, 178e, 181–183; self-images based on, 68; stories that give flesh to